"Provides effective, easy, thought-provoking, and fun activities that can begin or continue conversations with your children."
—California Association for the Gifted

"Hands-on enrichment activities that promote self-awareness, tolerance, character development, and service to others. Recommended."
—*Gifted Child Today*

GROWING GOOD KIDS

28 Activities to Enhance Self~Awareness, Compassion, and Leadership

Deb Delisle and Jim Delisle
Illustrations by **Ken Vinton**
Edited by **Marjorie Lisovskis**

free spirit
PUBLiSHiNG®

Helping kids
help themselves™
since 1983

Free Spirit, Free Spirit Publishing, and associated logos are trademarks and/or registered trademarks of Free Spirit Publishing Inc. A complete listing of our logos and trademarks is available at www.freespirit.com.

Library of Congress Cataloging-in-Publication Data

Delisle, Deb, 1953-

     Growing good kids: 28 activities to enhance self-awareness, compassion, and leadership / by Deb and Jim Delisle ; edited by Marjorie Lisovskis; [illustrations by Ken Vinton].

        p.   cm.

     Includes bibliographical references and index.

     ISBN 1-57542-009-0

     1.Creative activities and seat work. 2.Self-perception—Study and teaching. 3.Caring—Study and teaching. 4.Problem solving—Study and teaching. 5. Leadership—Study and teaching.

     I. Delisle, James R., 1953-   . II. Lisovskis, Marjorie. III. Title.

     LB1027.25.D45   1996   96-32528

     371.3'9—dc20   CIP

At the time of this book's publication, all facts and figures cited are the most current available. All telephone numbers, addresses, and Web site URLs are accurate and active; all publications, organizations, Web sites, and other resources exist as described in this book; and all have been verified as of March 2007. The authors and Free Spirit Publishing make no warranty or guarantee concerning the information and materials given out by organizations or content found at Web sites, and we are not responsible for any changes that occur after this book's publication. If you find an error or believe that a resource listed here is not as described, please contact Free Spirit Publishing. Parents, teachers, and other adults: We strongly urge you to monitor children's use of the Internet.

Permission is granted for teachers, counselors, and group leaders to photocopy the pages included in the "List of Reproducible Pages" (page vii) for individual classroom or group work only. Photocopying or other reproduction of these materials for an entire school or school system is strictly forbidden.

This book contains a number of examples of students' work. Their names have been changed for privacy.

The principles for invitational education on page 6 is from *Inviting School Success: A Self-Concept Approach to Teaching and Learning* by William W. Purkey and John M. Novak (Belmont, CA: Wadsworth Publishing, 1984), page 2.

Material on page 7 is from "Punished by Rewards? An Interview with Alfie Kohn" (*Educational Leadership*, vol. 53, no. 1, September 1995, page 14).

"Nile River Adventures" (pages 82-3) is adapted from *Kayaks Down the Nile* by John Goddard (Provo, UT: Brigham Young University Press, 1979), pages 12–13, 18–19, 110–11, and 136–37, with permission of the author.

"What's in a Game?" (page 147) is adapted from *TNT Teaching: Over 200 Dynamite Ways to Make Your Classroom Come Alive* by Randy Moberg (Minneapolis: Free Spirit Publishing Inc., 1994) with permission of the publisher.

"What to Wear?" (page 154) is from *I Felt Like I Was from Another Planet: Writing from Personal Experience* by Norine Dresser. Copyright © 1994 by Addison-Wesley Publishing Company. Reprinted by permission.

Book design by MacLean & Tuminelly

Index compiled by Eileen Quam and Theresa Wolner

15 14 13 12 11 10

Printed in the United States of America

FREE SPIRIT PUBLISHING INC.

217 Fifth Avenue North, Suite 200

Minneapolis, MN 55401-1299

(612) 338-2068

help4kids@freespirit.com

www.freespirit.com

Dedication

This book is dedicated to the thousands of students with whom we have worked. They have taught us about compassion and caring and have permitted us to help them become leaders. To each of them, we say "thanks" for helping both of us to grow a part of our hearts.

Most important, we also dedicate this book to our favorite kid, Matt. Every day, he continues to warm our hearts, lead us to new rainbows, and strengthen our belief that the future is, indeed, in good hands.

Contents

List of Reproducible Pages

Introduction

The difference between a goal and a dream is attitude. To the logical mind, a goal seems realistic. The term itself implies a predetermined point at which you know you've succeeded. A dream, on the other hand, relies on hunch and hope over logic; it is airier, but less bulky, than a goal. Its fulfillment depends more on vision and imagination than on planned, structured steps. More loosely defined than a goal, a dream tends to meander down uncharted paths. In fact, when a dream is reached, it may be a surprise even to the person who conceived it!

Our Goals and Our Dreams for Our Students

In our early years as educators, we often considered dreams and goals to be the same. Because of this, we did not always directly pursue our teaching goals (for fear that we would not succeed) and we tried to make our subjective dream of being good teachers too realistic. We thought, for example, that all our classroom lessons had to be as exciting and memorable as a Disney cartoon; when they weren't, we often saw ourselves as failures. By mixing up our goals for our students' learning with our dreams to be good teachers, we sidestepped many important lessons that would have benefited our students. These might not have been perfect lessons, but they would nonetheless have been good attempts.

It is only now, having taught long enough that many of our present students are the children of some of our earliest ones, that we have discovered the beauty in distinguishing our aims (goals) from our missions (dreams), in recognizing that learning occurs not only in the mind but also in the heart. Good things – like a sense of perspective on success or failure – do take time.

"To teach a child to read" may be our aim, but "to help a child appreciate the beauty of written words" is our mission. "Getting to know your community" is a laudable goal for our students, but "envisioning the possible ways you can serve your community" is a lifelong dream we seek for them. "Using higher level thinking skills" will expand children's minds; "developing empathy and concern for others" will open their hearts.

Our collective years in education have taught us a very important lesson: The most relevant and lasting learning experiences involve the heart. We'd like to think that classrooms everywhere would operate on the principle of designing "lessons of life." After all, long after our students have mastered the multiplication tables and memorized the capitals of the world, they will assume their roles as citizens. The most able mathematician, adroit political leader, articulate teacher, skilled surgeon, savvy business owner – each contributes more to society when applying technical and professional know-how from a foundation of self-confidence, compassion, respect for others, and stewardship.

As educators, we have both the opportunity and the obligation to prepare students fully to assume their roles as global citizens. How? By helping them to acquire academic skills and knowledge, certainly. Yet, equally important, by helping them appreciate themselves and care about others – and by providing concrete ways for them to act upon their caring.

Thus, this book, *Growing Good Kids*. Within its pages are many different examples of lessons we have designed and taught to help us reach our dream, our mission: to allow all students to experience the joy of learning about themselves while acting in the service of others.

About the Activities

In designing these lessons, we have paid attention to many solid principles of learning espoused by respected educators. All of the activities contain these elements:

They involve both cognitive and affective learning. The activities call on students to think, feel, and react simultaneously. Based mostly in the content areas of language arts and social studies, these activities also contain aspects of innovation, introspection, or humor – elements that help to make content memorable. For example, "Grate Misteaks" (pages 16–24) provides the cognitive lesson that mistakes sometimes lead to important inventions; it also invites students to explore the affective concept that none of us is perfect. In "Filling Our Own Shoes" (pages 70–72), students learn cognitively about individuals who had strength and character in their lives and reflect affectively on friends and family who have helped them build their own character.

They are experiential. Each activity is based upon the belief that our students already know much about life and themselves and that they are always curious to learn more. Too often, it is assumed that adults do the teaching while kids do the learning. In these activities, our goal is to blur this teaching-learning division by making learning an active, cooperative endeavor.

They are open-ended. All activities can be interpreted and completed according to the individual ideas of the teacher and the students. No child should feel reluctant to complete the work out of fear that the final product might be "wrong" or unacceptable. In fact, students will express themselves most creatively and benefit most fully when you allow them to complete the activities without regard to the almighty grade.

They are product focused. Every activity allows students to concretely demonstrate their thinking and feeling. Each lesson has a clearly defined beginning, middle, and end as well as a tangible product showing the results of students' explorations. In some cases, the product might be a piece of introspective writing (as in "I Wanna Be Bugged by You," pages 25–29); in others, it might be a community service project to help our global neighbors (as in "Links for Life," pages 122–126). Your students' conversations may suggest additional possibilities for products. "How can we share our learning?" is a question of great value for every activity.

They are teacher and student tested. We are not asking you to teach a lesson that we ourselves have not taught. Every activity has withstood the toughest test of all: a hands-on trial with students in "regular," heterogeneously grouped classroom settings. The samples of student work that accompany many lessons are just a handful of the many original, wise, and multifaceted responses the activities have elicited from children. The samples are intended as models and, as such, are excellent springboards for your students' creative endeavors. Share these examples with your students or use them for your own personal reference; the benefits of access to our students' work might encourage your students to stretch their minds and their hearts.

They can be modified to suit teachers' and students' special needs. Although the activities are broadly designed for heterogeneously grouped classrooms of students in grades 3–8, teachers at the primary or high school levels should be able to adjust many of the activities with little trouble. Likewise, we recognize that every classroom has its own unique personality. We encourage you to mold and reshape the activities in consideration of and respect for your students' needs, strengths, interests, and weaknesses (yes, even these!). Remember, no single book is appropriate for all students of any age. Pick and choose appropriately, for you know your students better than anyone.

They are flexible in scope and time. Each activity has been designed so that you can adapt it to your own and your students' needs. You'll find that some activities will work best within individual classrooms. Others will be equally effective in a large team setting of multiple classrooms. Still others are appropriate for schoolwide participation.

Some lessons are intended for one class session, while others may extend for longer periods of time. In each instance, we'll tell you the most effective time frame we've found for conducting the lessons. Feel free to adapt this to your own particular situation. Read through the activity and determine what goals are important for your students, then match them within a workable time frame that fits your schedule as well as your instructional style. After all, learning involves taking risks and using information in different ways.

They can be holistically evaluated. In the process of "growing good kids," the issue of grading students' work also arises. The purpose of the activities, as designed and field tested, is to enhance self-awareness, expand leadership opportunities, and generate creativity and compassion. As such, the activities are not intended to be evaluated with an arbitrary letter or number grade. Doing so will give students too little direction in how to improve their work and may stifle their blossoming sense of self and awareness of others. A gentle reminder: These activities are meant to open student's minds and hearts. Be cautious – children are "growing."

How to Use the Activities

Each activity begins with a brief introduction followed by capsulized information about learning objectives, product, related curriculum areas, materials, time frame, and, if necessary, preparation guidelines. A few activities provide useful background information as well. Activity steps are clearly numbered. Most activities include "For Surefire Success" hints for making the activity fully effective. You will also find suggestions for adapting or expanding many activities for use with your own class, other classes, students' families, and the community.

With some activities, we suggest related books and other resources that may be of interest to you or your students. You will find descriptions, publishing information, and where-to-find-it facts about these optional materials in "Resources We Recommend" (pages 11–14).

While most of the activities include a writing component, feel free to substitute other means of communication (audio, video, drawing, skits, and so on) if you'd rather not assign a writing activity or if some of your students have difficulty writing.

Holistic Evaluation

What It Is

Comments that:

give second chances to improve

consider the paper or product as a whole

offer constructive ideas for growth and improvement

ask the student, "What did you learn?"

What It Isn't

Letter/number grades that:

say, "One strike, you're out!"

dissect individual segments

provide little, if any, constructive feedback on strengths and weaknesses

ask the student, "What did you earn?"

The sequence for using the activities is entirely up to you. Start by choosing those that spark your interest or that seem particularly fitting for your group of students. A few activities will work especially well at the beginning of the school year. The [symbol] symbol signals these "get-acquainted" activities. You will also find these activities helpful when there have been changes in the makeup of your classroom and when people need to get "reacquainted" after holiday or term breaks.

Time frames reflect our experience using the activities. These will vary depending on the size of your class or group, the ages of your students, the time of day, and your own teaching style. You may find it helpful to plan your own time frame for each activity step.

We'd Love to Hear from You

Please let us know how the activities work for you. Did you modify them to fit your personal style, talents, or school circumstances? If so, how? What changes can you suggest? We also invite you to send us some of your students' responses to the activities. We'd love to correspond with you and your students about how you like the activities — and, yes, we *will* write back! Write to us in care of Free Spirit Publishing, 217 Fifth Avenue North, Suite 200, Minneapolis, MN 55401-1299.

Remember, we're all in this thing called "education" together. Together we can surely broaden our students' hearts and minds and, in doing so, fulfill our own goals and dreams! After all, what better beginning can we give our students for life than the gift of learning to "grow" their own hearts? Everyone's future depends on our "growing good kids." We hope this book becomes a valued resource in your classroom.

Deb and Jim Delisle
Kent, Ohio

Creating an Invitational Classroom and School

Remember the classroom rules that met you on your first day of school each year? Sometimes the rules were short and to the point. At other times they went on for pages, compiled by teachers who apparently never considered the idea that "less is more." Whether the rules were brief or seemingly endless, they probably had words like these in common: "don't," "no," and "never."

Don't talk out of turn.

No food in class.

Never run in the halls.

There was very little encouragement to do anything positive; rather, you were surrounded by warnings of what *not* to do. Unfortunately, this remains true for many students today. Consider a day as uninviting as this:

Sandy waits in a cold rain for a school bus that is already 20 minutes late. As the bus pulls up, water sprays her new jeans. Climbing onto the bus, she's greeted with the driver's gruff, "C'mon – I'm not your private chauffeur, you know. Hurry up!" As Sandy takes her seat, the kids sitting two rows back start taunting her by calling her "Wet Pants." She tries to ignore them, but it's not easy.

The first person she meets upon arrival at school is the custodian, who warns the students not to drip on the just-waxed floor. Sandy scurries by to avoid detection. Once at her desk, she looks up at the board and reads, "Homework that is not turned in by the opening bell earns a grade of zero." Guess what? The three pages of homework that Sandy worked on last weekend for two hours are nowhere to be found.

The school day begins. Misbehaving students get their names written on the board, with a check mark for each additional offense. Sandy sees that one more check mark next to Brian's name will mean no recess for the entire class!

The class makes it to recess somehow. As students choose teams for kickball, it's clear that no one wants Sandy. As usual, she's chosen last, and her teammates groan as she joins them. Then, for no reason at all, one student from her team punches another one, forcing a schoolyard monitor to intervene. "When you go inside," says the monitor, "you will each write 'I will not fight at recess' 10 times. I expect to see your sentences before recess tomorrow."

With the day almost over, Sandy can't wait to go home. Just before dismissal, her teacher announces the results of last Friday's math test. When she hears "Sandy – C, 72 percent," Sandy grabs her paper, embarrassed, and ducks back into her seat.

The bus ride home is quiet. Hardly anyone is in the mood for talking.

For Sandy, school is a constant series of uninviting hurdles, a minefield of potential embarrassments waiting to explode. In an environment so mired in negativity, what is there to sustain students' long-term interest? Of course, Sandy's scenario is extreme. Yet the negative impact of a day even half as bad as Sandy's will eventually take its toll on most students.

Invite Learning with a Positive Climate

Now consider how we could invite students like Sandy to cooperate and succeed in school. Imagine a classroom with rules like these:

> ### Classroom Rules
> 1. Walking in the halls prevents accidents.
> 2. Be mature and serious during fire drills.
> 3. Enjoy chewing your gum at home.
> 4. When in groups, talk in 6-inch voices.
> 5. Ask before you use.
> 6. People can be hurt by words and actions, so use both carefully.
>
> Please remember: Kindness is contagious!

Focusing on what students *already do right* and on what they *may do* fosters a productive and dynamic classroom and school. Students recognize what the school personnel value. As teachers, we need to assume that students want to learn. We can expect that when we give them reasonable amounts of challenge and freedom, students will behave appropriately in our classrooms. If we truly communicate these positive expectations, many of our worries about classroom management will evaporate. Further, we will do more than set an expectation for cooperation; we'll establish an *invitation* to students to take part in a truly cooperative learning experience.

One of the strongest advocates of "invitational education" is an educator named William Purkey. In *Inviting School Success: A Self-Concept Approach to Teaching and Learning,* he and John Novak discuss the links between students' attitudes toward school and their school success. Purkey and Novak stress four principles for invitational education:

1. People are able, valuable, and responsible and should be treated accordingly.

2. Teaching should be a cooperative activity.

3. People possess relatively untapped potential in all areas of human development.

4. This potential can best be realized by places, policies, and programs that are specifically designed to invite development and by people who are personally and professionally inviting to themselves and others.

When we invite students to become partners in their own and their classmates' learning, they recognize that we anticipate success and cooperation rather than negative behavior.

There are many ways schools can implement invitational education. Purkey and Novak's book is a gold mine of ideas for doing so. The "inviters" need not be only the teachers whose jobs involve direct and sustained daily contact with students. As the example of Sandy suggests, all people in any school community – including the principal, office personnel, cafeteria workers, custodians, librarian, media and resource aides, and bus drivers – play important roles in making a school the kind of place where learning and belonging go hand in hand.

Invite Schoolwide Commitment to Fostering a Positive Learning Environment

Some principles of invitational education involve discipline and classroom environments; others focus more on curriculum content and instructional practices. For example, a school with a policy against all forms of acceleration dismisses the talents of a second grader whose math skills are at a fifth-grade competency. On the other hand, a school where learning is individualized to the point where children flow freely from teacher to teacher, depending on their unique levels of ability, allows students to tap into their talents without regard to grade-level placement. Is it more difficult to operate a school based on the latter approach? Of course, but it is our responsibility as educators to do the job necessary to fully promote student achievement.

Work with your colleagues to examine your school and district for policies and practices that may inhibit learning or positive behaviors. Together, arrive at alternative methods of promoting achievement and good discipline by implementing ideas that anticipate the positive over the negative.

Invite Effort by Involving and Motivating Students

A common practice of classroom management, and one that would seem in concert with the goals of invitational education, is that of praising students for good behavior and performance. Too much praise or too many rewards, however, teach students to work for the wrong reasons.

In *Punished by Rewards,* Alfie Kohn argues convincingly that many teachers are too ready to reward children for relatively minor or superficial improvements in work or behavior. By doing so, he contends, educators manipulate children's behavior, diminishing their potential for real learning.

Here's Kohn's hypothesis: Setting up a classroom on the basis of "if you do *this* you will get *that*" does not really motivate students to make an effort, to behave well, or to want to learn. On the contrary, the message to students is that they will be rewarded for doing what is *expected* of them. There are times, in fact, when rewards or praise are actually punitive. For example, consider Tobias:

At the beginning of the geography lesson, the teacher says to the class, "I like the way Tobias is sitting and ready to work." Tobias cringes, and with good reason. He can already foresee the problems the teacher's comment will bring about. Other students will resent him and let him know it! He can well imagine the jeers he'll receive, all along the lines of, "Whoa, Tobias! Mr. 'Nice and Quiet' Dork!" The teacher's focus on Tobias puts other students in competition with him, a competition Tobias does not want at all. In effect, manipulating Tobias to control the behavior of the other students makes him a pawn. With the best of intentions, the teacher has punished Tobias for his good behavior!

Often, too, the praise or reward intended to elicit good behavior has no useful connection to the desired behavior. For example, a desktop jar with marbles that represent times the teacher "catches a student being good" may earn a pizza party at the end of the month. However, the connection between the pizza and the specific acts that led to this treat are, at best, tenuous. The connection between the pizza and learning appropriate behavior is even less clear.

When teachers praise good grades orally ("There were five A's in math today – I'm so proud of those students!") or with stars and stickers, there is seldom mention of the level of effort, if any, that went into getting the grades. Thus, a student who does very little thinking but nonetheless earns an A also earns praise for minimal effort. Most students recognize the emptiness of this kind of praise, while the efforts of students who worked hard for a B or C go virtually unnoticed. When teachers give praise and rewards indiscriminately, they unintentionally take away students' internal motivation to achieve something personally valuable.

We agree with Kohn's suggestion that a preferable alternative to praise is to provide curriculum options that are personally involving and motivating. Students challenged in this way will want to complete the work out of an intrinsic desire to learn more about something interesting. When such conditions exist, there is no need to provide artificial rewards. The best and truest rewards of all are the feelings of joy and accomplishment that accompany a fulfilling learning experience. Kohn suggests addressing these "Three Cs":

Content. Have students been given something to do that is worth learning? As Kohn so aptly notes, the answer to the question "Which is bigger, $\frac{5}{7}$ or $\frac{9}{11}$?" is "Who cares?" A personalized question is far more compelling: "If you were ravenously hungry and were given the choice of $\frac{5}{7}$ or $\frac{9}{11}$ of a pizza, which would you choose?" In this case, many of us would care very much!

Community. It's essential that students know they are part of a safe environment in which they feel free to ask for help. Also, when students feel a sense of belonging, they see themselves as partners, not competitors, in the learning process.

Choice. Having choices helps students feel both valued and responsible. Students need to have some options, about not only what to learn and how to learn it, but also with whom to learn it. The value of offering students choices became clear to Deb early in her teaching career, when she learned that even the best-designed units of study needed to be reshaped.

During an introductory activity to a unit on butterflies, Deb asked her third graders to tell her everything they knew about the topic. After 15 minutes it became clear that the majority of lessons she'd planned covered facts the students already knew. Deb needed to decide immediately between two options: to continue with a unit that would be repetitive, or to ask the students what questions they had about butterflies that they could answer during the unit. After writing approximately 20 student questions on the board, Deb asked her students to sign up individually for those questions they would tackle as part of the unit. If Deb hadn't offered these choices, her class would have missed out on a very stirring poem written by Rachel and Ira, "Where Do Butterflies Go When It Rains?"

The activities in *Growing Good Kids* are designed with Kohn's "Three Cs" in mind. Our aim is to foster in students both their intrinsic desire to learn and their positive emotional development.

Invite Risk Taking by Allowing Mistakes

Quick! Name one thing that every one of us has in common but nearly all of us like to keep hidden from everyone else.

Give up? Take a guess. It's okay if you guess wrong and make a mistake; in fact, mistakes are the point. The common thread that weaves through our collective lives is the human frailty we all share: the propensity to make mistakes again, and again, and again.

Of course, most of us don't like to admit to being less than perfect – factory seconds in a world of designer originals. But, truth be known, we all are just a little bit off base, at least some of the time.

Think about it: Star athletes successfully complete just a fraction of their passes or stolen bases. Television and movie actors audition for dozens of parts before getting a role. Renowned scientists take years to perfect one formula or theorem, ever conscious that each "error" provides one more example of how something *doesn't* work. If it's acceptable for our highest paid and most esteemed citizens to make mistakes like these, shouldn't it be acceptable for the kids in our classrooms, too?

Some of the activities in this book allow you to emphasize the idea that mistakes are actually a good thing. Here are some other ways to show your students that mistakes are a necessary and acceptable part of learning:

Display imperfect work. Post on your walls and bulletin boards student work that, while good, is not perfect. Posting only perfection sends the wrong message. Highlight this work with a catchy slogan. You may wish to ask students themselves to select and post work they are especially proud of, even if it is a tad imperfect.

Admit your own mistakes. Share with your students your own instances of mistake making. Revisit the memory of going the wrong way down a one-way street. Recount the time you held your spouse's hand at the zoo only to discover that it was somebody (or something) else's hand you were clasping. These situations humanize you in ways that students don't forget.

Make intentional mistakes. Put an intentional error on a test or homework assignment, awarding an extra point to students who find and correct it. (Be prepared to have them find mistakes you weren't aware of, too!)

It may seem like a small thing to extol the virtues of making mistakes. However, to students who are especially conscious of their own academic, social, and physical imperfections, your willingness to go public with something that most teachers keep to themselves will send a strong message of support to kids who need it the most.

So go ahead and break a leg (figuratively speaking, of course)!

The ABCs of Effective Learning Environments

A ctively involve your students in planning their learning activities and outcomes.

B ecome an advocate for inquiry-based education, where students discover new facets about both themselves and their world.

C oncentrate on small steps and successes. Demonstrate your own **C**ompassion.

D ecide to make at least one major change in your teaching style each year.

E njoy the lessons as much as your students do. **E**ngage your students in active learning.

F acilitate meaningful discussions among your students.

G ather many resources for use in planning and carrying out units of study.

H elp all students tap into their own talents and interests.

I ntroduce at least one new unit of study per school year.

J ust relax and enjoy your students as they are – not for what you'd like them to become.

K now your students, their needs, and their interests.

L ove teaching. This will automatically transfer to your actions.

M ake time for every student.

N egotiate classroom rules with your students.

O ften reflect on your educational philosophies, teaching practices, and daily actions.

P eriodically take time to let your students "breathe": **P**lan an "off day" when you divert from the curriculum to simply have fun with learning activities.

Q uestion practices that have become second nature to you.

R espond to students with **R**espect.

S hare your enthusiasm with your students, their parents, and your colleagues. **S**mile a lot.

T ake time to enjoy life's small gifts with your students: the first snowfall, colored leaves in autumn, the first flower in the spring, a rainbow.

U se what you feel in your heart as you plan learning activities.

V alidate every student at least once a week. Greet students by name, ask them to help you, notice their efforts, tell them you enjoy them.

W rite often, **W**onder much, and **WO**W your students every day.

EX pect that every student will succeed. **EX**perience learning a new skill with your students.

Y earn to make your classroom an exciting place in which to learn.

Z ero in on those learning activities that actively involve students and cause them to want to return to your classroom tomorrow.

Above all, never quit. Keep a caring heart and an open mind, and you and your students will grow together!

Resources We Recommend

Following are descriptions, publishing information, and where-to-find-it facts for the resources we recommend in the individual activities, plus a few more worth checking out.

- Albert, Linda. *Cooperative Discipline*. (Circle Pines, MN: American Guidance Service, 1996.)

    What are some nonthreatening, noncoercive ways you can compel your students to behave and get along with their classmates? This excellent resource gives you hundreds of possible solutions that allow students to maintain their dignity when classroom problems arise. Albert also offers positive strategies for fostering cooperation, personal responsibility, and a sense of belonging.

- Baum, L. Frank *The Wizard of Oz*. (Austin, TX: Holt, Rinehart and Winston, 1982.)

    The original edition of this book was published in 1900 under the title *The Wonderful Wizard of Oz*. Many versions have been published over the years. The familiar movie adaptation is available on video. Check the video out of your school's media center or your local video rental store.

- Baylor, Byrd, illustrated by Peter Parnall. *I'm in Charge of Celebrations*. (New York: Scribner Books for Young Readers, 1986.)

    Imagine if there were a "Rainbow Celebration Day," a "Coyote Day," or a "New Year Celebration" that began on April 24. In this book, that's exactly what you get, as a young girl imagines all the reasons to celebrate in her desert home. Great ideas for creative and introspective thinking by students!

- Brodkin, Margaret, and the Coleman Advocates. *Every Kid Counts: Thirty-One Ways to Save Our Children*. (San Francisco: Harper, 1993.)

    This wonderful book gives specific ideas, resources, and organizations that kids can use to become more active in addressing community or global issues such as poverty, the environment, health, and education.

- Brown, H. Jackson, Jr. *Live and Learn and Pass It On*. (Nashville, TN: Rutledge Hill Press, 1992.)

    A book of one-liners. This short volume details nuances about life that are well worth knowing.

    ———. *Wit and Wisdom from the Peanut Butter Gang*. (Nashville, TN: Rutledge Hill Press, 1994.)

    This book is filled with one-sentence thoughts ("When a teacher is in a bad mood, there's no way I'm going to ask to go to the bathroom," p. 42) and illustrations by children who give advice on living life well. Humor and poignancy are evident throughout.

- Burack, Jonathan, ed. *Editorial Cartoons by Kids*. (Madison, WI: Knowledge Unlimited, 2002.)

    This book's publisher used to sponsor an editorial cartoon contest for students in grades 3–12, publishing the winning entries in book form. A great way to review recent history! Write to Knowledge Unlimited, P.O. Box 52, Madison, WI 53701-0052. Toll-free telephone: 1-800-356-2303.

- Cooney, Barbara. *Miss Rumphius*. (New York: Viking Children's Books, 1982.)

  Once, long ago, Miss Rumphius was a little girl named Alice who lived in a place by the sea. She had many dreams and goals, but her wise grandfather reminded her that she *must* do "something to make the world more beautiful." This award-winning picture book shows you how Miss Rumphius goes about doing just that.

- *Creative Kids*.

  A bimonthly publication devoted entirely to publishing student writing, art, games, and puzzles. You might submit your students' writing and artwork that result from activities in *Growing Good Kids*. The editors communicate promptly regarding submissions. Call for a sample issue or write to Prufrock Press, P.O. Box 8813, Waco, TX 76714-8813. Toll-free telephone: 1-800-998-2208.

- Delisle, Jim. *Kidstories: Biographies of 20 Young People You'd Like to Know*. (Minneapolis: Free Spirit Publishing Inc., 1991.)

  Biographies do not have to be about famous dead people. This book gives students a chance to see that everyday heroes exist all around them, even in class.

- Dresser, Norine. *I Felt Like I Was from Another Planet: Writing from Personal Experience*. (Reading, MA: Addison-Wesley Publishing, 1994.)

  Recently arrived teenage immigrants from throughout the world recall how awkward they felt when put into unfamiliar American situations. A remarkable book that teaches both the beauty of diverse cultures and the uncomfortable moments often experienced by those unfamiliar with them.

- Fox, Mem, illustrated by Julie Vivas. *Wilfrid Gordon McDonald Partridge*. (Brooklyn, NY: Kane/Miller Book Publishers, 1989.)

  When a young boy visits an elderly neighbor who has "lost" her memory, Wilfrid decides to find it for her. This heartwarming story of intergenerational love will prompt much discussion among your students.

- *Games Magazine*.

  Great ideas for creative and logical thinking! This bimonthly magazine offers dozens of intriguing puzzles and games guaranteed to stump even the most methodical thinkers. Available at newsstands everywhere. Or write to Kappa Publishing Group, 6198 Butler Pike, Suite 200, Blue Bell, PA 19422. Telephone: (815) 734-1212.

- Garrison, Jennifer, and Andrew Tubesing. *A Million Visions of Peace: Wisdom from the Friends of Old Turtle*. (Duluth, MN: Pfeifer-Hamilton, 1996.)

  This little book contains a collection of expressions of peace gathered from children and adults across the U.S. Simple, touching, and eloquent, the messages are timeless expressions of hope. A book to cherish.

- Hoffman, Mary, illustrated by Caroline Binch. *Amazing Grace*. (New York: Dial Books for Young Readers, 1991.)

  The story of a young African-American girl who wants to act the part of Peter Pan in her school play, even though people tell her she can't because she is a girl and because she is black. A compelling story about the power of positive thinking, self-confidence, and strong role models.

- Johnessee, Judith A. "A Boy and His Cat." *Reader's Digest* (July, 1995): 145–146.

  A heartrending short story, written by a veterinarian, on how she helps a 14-year-old boy cope with and understand the death of his beloved pet cat.

- Jones, Charlotte Foltz, illustrated by John O'Brien. *Mistakes That Worked*. (New York: Doubleday, 1991.)

  Coca-Cola, Post-it Notes, Frisbees, cheese, chocolate chip cookies, and aspirin — all are inventions that happened by accident. This delightful book gives new meaning to the word "oops" as it explores the beauty of not being perfect and of using creativity to make the best of a bad situation. We've used some of the inventions Jones describes as the basis for the "Grate Misteaks" activity (see pages 16–24).

- Kane, Pearl E., ed. *The First Year of Teaching: Real World Stories from America's Teachers.* (New York: NAL/Dutton, 1992.)

  Twenty-five essays written by teachers who recall their first year of teaching. Touching, funny, poignant – we've all been there! This is a perfect gift for a student teacher.

- Kohn, Alfie. *Punished by Rewards.* (New York: Houghton Mifflin, 1993.)

  Put away your stickers and your desktop marble jars! According to Kohn, rewards like stickers and marbles send the wrong message to students as they take away the intrinsic desire to learn and replace it with empty external rewards. Controversial, to be sure, but worth a good, long read.

- Krensky, Beth, ed. *Kids Share Their Lives through Poetry, Art, and Photography.* (Weston, MA: Font and Center Press, 1995.)

  This honest and refreshing book captures the imaginations and spirits of 57 kids ages 6–14 years. A heartfelt collection of poetry, art, and pictures, it will stir everyone into thinking about the notion of peace. An excellent resource for kids of all ages and for their teachers and parents. For sure, it will generate some moving discussions in your classroom.

- Levine, Michael. *The Address Book: How to Reach Anyone Who Is Anyone*, 7th rev. ed. (New York: Perigree Books, 1995.)

  Every famous person lives somewhere, and this book tells you where. Updated annually (as is its complementary volume, *The Kids' Address Book*), *The Address Book* is an invaluable resource if you plan to write to actors, singers, artists, authors, CEOs, or other famous folks.

- Manes, Stephen. *Be a Perfect Person in Just Three Days.* (New York: Bantam Books, 1987.)

  Caught up with the urge to be perfect in social and academic ways, a young boy learns the beauty of making mistakes from a wise and wacky professor. A great read-aloud book. (Also available as a video. Check it out of your school's media center or your local video rental store.)

- Moberg, Randy. *TNT Teaching: Over 200 Dynamite Ways to Make Your Classroom Come Alive.* (Minneapolis: Free Spirit Publishing Inc., 1994.)

  This book offers a wealth of creative ideas for both new and seasoned teachers. The "Design-a-Game Kit" on pages 137–46 can be of great help for your "Games to Go" activity (see pages 144–150).

- Purkey, William W., and John M. Novak. *Inviting School Success: A Self-Concept Approach to Teaching and Learning.* (Belmont, CA: Wadsworth Publishing, 1984.)

  If we could recommend only one book on how to become a more effective and sensitive teacher, this would be it. Purkey and Novak suggest hundreds of practical ways to make school more like a "family" and less like a "factory."

- *Random Acts of Kindness*, by the editors of Conari Press. (Emeryville, CA: Conari Press, 1993.)

  Oprah has helped make this book a bestseller. Between its covers is a collection of short essays about people helping people for no reason other than shared humanity. Also of interest is *Kids' Random Acts of Kindness* (Conari Press, 1994), though we suggest you have your students create their own kids' book (see "The Footpath of Peace," pages 104–106).

- Seuss, Dr. (Theodor Seuss Geisel). *Green Eggs and Ham* video.

  One segment, "The Sneetches," explores what happens when a group of people has something that everyone else envies. Great for discussions of what is really important in life. Check this video out of your school's media center or your local video rental store.

  ———. *Oh, the Places You'll Go!* (New York: Random Books for Young Readers, 1993.)

  A fitting gift to give at graduation or transition points in anyone's life, this creative, thoughtful book will make you appreciate the beauty and fear that accompany change.

————. *The Sneetches and Other Stories*. (New York: Random Books for Young Readers, 1961.)

> When an entrepreneur moves into town with a machine that puts stars on your belly, all the residents want one – but they can't all have one. What results is a classic no-win situation where competition and greed win out over common sense and cooperation. A marvelous story for young and old alike!

- Suid, Murray, and Roberta Suid. *Happy Birthday to U.S.: Activities for the Bicentennial*. (Menlo Park: CA: Addison-Wesley, 1975.)

> If the "Possible Dreams" activity (pages 80–87) leaves you or your students curious to know more about anthropologist and adventurer John Goddard, you'll find a complete list of his original 127 goals and daydreams in this book (page 54).

- *Teaching Tolerance*.

> A free biannual magazine filled with stories and ideas about how thoughtful people are making the world a kinder place. *The Shadow of Hate*, a video on the history of intolerance in America, is also free and available from the magazine's publisher. (View it before showing — it's tough stuff.) Write to the Southern Poverty Law Center, 400 Washington Avenue, Montgomery, AL 36104. Telephone: (334) 956-8200.

- Terban, Marvin, illustrated by Giulio Maelstro. *Mad As a Wet Hen! And Other Funny Idioms*. (New York: Clarion Books, 1987.)

> In this book, students learn both the meanings of idioms and how they came to be a part of our language and culture. A great resource for showing kids that reading, writing, and speaking can be fun!

- Thaler, Mike. *Teacher from the Black Lagoon*. (New York: Scholastic, 1989.)

> What happens on the first day of school when the teacher, Mrs. Green, turns out to be a *real* dragon lady? This is a hilarious story about beginning-of-the-school-year fears.

- Viorst, Judith. *If I Were in Charge of the World and Other Worries*. (New York: Aladdin Books, 1984.)

> Humorous and thought-provoking poetry written from the vantage point of a curious and feisty 12-year-old girl. Lots of good discussion starters!

The following books are out of print, but well worth sharing with your students. Check your school, community, and local university library collections to see if any of these titles are available.

- Goddard, John. *Kayaks Down the Nile*. (Provo, UT: Brigham Young University Press, 1979.)

> The pictures and diary entries of a world-class explorer who chose to do something no one had ever done before. We've excerpted episodes from this exciting true-adventure story in the "Possible Dreams" activity (see pages 82–83).

- Gustafson, Scott. *Alphabet Soup: A Feast of Letters*. (Chicago: Contemporary Books, 1990.)

> The otter is having supper for his friends, and every one of them brings an ingredient that begins with a different alphabet letter. Beautifully written and illustrated, this picture book will enchant reluctant readers and older children alike. It is a perfect book to share with students as part of the "ABCs of Our Lives" activity (see pages 30–41).

- Hammond, Dave. *Plexers* and *More Plexers*. (Palo Alto, CA: Dale Seymour Publishing, 1983.)

> These books present hundreds of humorous and thought-provoking word pictures, such as "SpKieY" ("pie in the sky") and "he art" ("broken heart"). You and your students will find them helpful for creative writing and for the study of many idioms. We share the books with students when we conduct the activity "The Great Idiom Contest" (see pages 130–135).

Activities for Growing with Myself and Others

Grate Misteaks

Most students are all too aware of their own mistakes. Not all children, however, realize that adults are as mistake-prone as young people. Even more surprising is the discovery that mistakes have led to the invention of products and tools that are integral parts of our daily lives.

Using the historical invention of cheese described in Charlotte Jones's *Mistakes That Worked,* take your students on an excursion into the "Land of Oops" – the place where accidental discoveries turn into creations with a purpose. Then, in an effort to help students appreciate both the inevitability and the benefits of making mistakes, join them in revisiting and reassessing some of their own most embarrassing moments.

Learning Objectives

Through this activity, students will:

*   think critically and creatively
*   recognize the value of mistakes in the creative process
*   find humor in their own and others' mistakes
*   understand that mistakes are inevitable and acceptable
*   tell and write personal anecdotes

Product

Student-created bulletin board dedicated to the students' (and the teacher's) greatest mistakes

Related Curriculum

Language Arts, Social Studies, Science

Materials

*   paper bag or pillowcase containing a chocolate chip cookie, a piece of Silly Putty, a Frisbee, a can of Coca-Cola, and a packet of Post-it Notes
*   overhead projector and transparency made from "Students' Grate Misteaks" reproducible master (pages 20–21) *or* copies for each student
*   copies of "My Greatest Mistake" handout (page 22) for each student
*   pencils, colored pencils, pens, crayons, or markers

Optional: *Mistakes That Worked* by Charlotte Foltz Jones

For Classroom Extensions: transparency made from "Major League Mistakes" reproducible master (pages 23–24) or copies for each student; *Be a Perfect Person in Just Three Days* by Stephen Manes (book or video)

For School Extension: camera and film

Time

One 45-minute session

Activity Steps

1. Introduce the activity. Begin by asking students to complete this statement: "The greatest inventor of all time is _____." You can expect answers ranging from Marie Curie, George Washington Carver, and Thomas Edison to "the person who invented the computer" and "whoever thought up MTV."

"Good answers!" you may respond, "but they're all wrong!" Then reveal the answer, attributed to Mark Twain, that the greatest inventor of all time is "Accident."

Your students will probably look puzzled, so go on to prove your point with this story: "It was a long, hot day and a long, hot ride. The camel had bad breath and great aim when he spat at his rider, who rode along uncomfortably on his shifting, jerky perch. It's a good thing the traveler had milk in his pouch to quench his thirst. But when he opened the pouch to drink some milk, a funny thing had happened. Can you guess what it was?"

Don't be surprised if several students get the answer right: The milk had turned into cheese. (It was the shaking up and down of the milk, coupled with the enzymatic action of the animal-stomach pouch, that curdled the milk.)

2. Tell about inventions that resulted from mistakes. Take out your bag or pillowcase. Read some or all of the following descriptions. As students guess what the invention was, pull the item out for all to see. The inventions are also described in the book *Mistakes That Worked*.

- Ruth Wakefield was running around trying to clean and cook for the guests staying at her inn in Massachusetts when she realized she'd forgotten to make a dessert for dinner. "No problem," she thought, "I'll make chocolate cookies." She searched her kitchen for baking chocolate (the dark, bitter kind), but all she had were milk chocolate candy bars. She hurriedly broke up the candy bars and tossed the pieces into the cookie dough. What did Ruth Wakefield invent? *(Chocolate chip cookies. Students may know them as Toll House cookies, named*

after Ruth Wakefield's rooming house, The Toll House Inn.)

- During World War II, real rubber was scarce, so the U.S. government asked scientists to invent artificial rubber. James Wright experimented with silicone and boric acid, but all he got was a lump of stuff that was too flexible and bouncy to be made into tires or army boots. He thought he had failed completely. Several years later, Peter Hodgson saw the advantages of Wright's "failed" experiment. What very silly thing had James Wright invented? *(Silly Putty)*

- In Bridgeport, Connecticut, there was a bakery known for its delicious pies. Each pie came baked in its own metal dish. Students at nearby Yale University loved these pies – and the dishes, for when the students were done eating, they now had a toy. They'd toss the pie dish from person to person in an odd game of catch. Whoever threw the pie dish called out the name of the bakery imprinted on it. What was the name of the bakery and the toy? *(Frisbee)*

- Dr. John Pemberton invented a hair dye and a couple of potions that made you go to the toilet more, or less, often. While he was formulating a medicine to get rid of nervousness and headaches, he decided it needed a little water and ice. By accident, his assistant added the wrong water – carbonated instead of from the tap. What did Dr. Pemberton and his assistant invent? *(Coca-Cola)*

- A large manufacturer needed a really strong glue to compete with Krazy Glue. One scientist had the *almost* perfect formula, but his glue was too weak to hold anything together permanently. Four years later, another scientist from the same company was singing in a church choir. He kept losing his place in the hymnal as all of his page markers fell to the floor. It was then that he thought of the weak glue, and a great way to use it. What new product did the scientists invent? *(Post-it Notes)*

Once you have finished this demonstration, ask your students to explain the point of these stories: A mistake isn't always a bad thing if you view it in a different way. Sometimes you have to make mistakes before you learn something new.

3. Talk about personal mistakes. Tell your students about a mistake in your own life, an embarrassing moment that you'll never forget. (This is where the real fun begins! Our favorite is when Jim had just finished telling students to be *sure* to choose dry-erase markers to use on the new, white marker boards. Within 10 minutes, he had covered an entire marker board with sentences and diagrams, using a permanent black marker!)

Ask your students if they've ever made a mistake that left them feeling silly or embarrassed. You might ask:

- Did you ever score a goal or basket for the other team? What happened? How did you feel?

- Did you ever talk to someone you thought was your friend, only to find out you were talking to a total stranger? What happened? How did you feel?

- Did you ever put your clothes on inside out, or forget to wear something you should have worn, like a bathing suit? What happened? How did you feel?

- Did you ever say something behind a teacher's back, only to discover that the teacher heard you? What happened? How did you feel?

- Did you ever make a mistake that turned out not to be a mistake after all? What happened? How did you feel?

Allow several volunteers to tell their stories. Once the laughter subsides, ask:

- What did you learn from your mistakes?

Next, explain that the class is going to compile a bulletin board called "Our Gratest Misteaks," in which students (and the teacher) reveal some of their most embarrassing moments.

4. Write about mistakes. Display or distribute "Students' Grate Misteaks." Read the descriptions of mistakes and discuss them together. Then distribute the "My Greatest Mistake" handout and have children write and, if they wish, illustrate their "gratest misteak." If students have trouble thinking of their own mistakes, suggest that they write about one made by a family member. Caution students against revealing anything too personal or embarrassing. Refer back to the "Students' Grate Misteaks" samples to spark your students' thinking.

5. Display stories about mistakes. Post the written accounts, including your own, for all to see. You have just taught your students a lifelong lesson: Mistakes happen to every one of us and we can often learn something from them.

Classroom Extensions

- Using "Major League Mistakes" as a springboard, have students research the mistakes and setbacks of famous people. Or have students write letters to parents, business and community leaders, or national figures asking them what important mistakes they made in their lives and what they learned from them. (*The Address Book* by Michael Levine, published annually, lists the addresses of hundreds of famous people.) Students can write or tell about what the mistakes were and how they affected the people's lives.

- View the video or read the book *Be a Perfect Person in Just Three Days* by Stephen Manes. This is a hilarious set of misadventures attempted by a young boy for whom looking good and being right is essential. Have a discussion about the stress caused when we strive to be perfect.

- Design a series of bumper stickers or posters to hang around the school extolling the virtues of mistakes. Some examples: "Less than perfect is more than acceptable." "I can't remember any mistakes I've made." "Nothing succeeds like attempts."

School Extension

Take a photograph of each teacher and staff member. Post the photos on a bulletin board, next to descriptions of memorable mistakes these adults made in life. Kids will thoroughly enjoy having adults "humanized" in this way!

Family Extension

On open house night, place fresh copies of the "My Greatest Mistake" handout on students' desks or tables. Ask parents and other visitors to anonymously write down mistakes they've made in their lives. At the end of the evening, collect the handouts. The next day, have the students read the visitors' responses and post these embarrassing (but fun) moments on a bulletin board.

Variations

- Instead of a bulletin board, compile mistakes in individual or class booklets.

- Encourage students to use a small notebook to keep a "Learning Log" in which they record mistakes that have either turned out *not* to be mistakes or have taught students something good or important. At the end of the year, have an informal sharing of these "grate misteaks" along with cookies and punch.

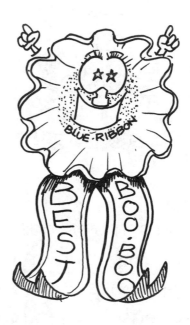

Students' Grate Misteaks

Here are some fifth and sixth graders' "grate misteaks." What do you think these students learned from their "misteaks"?

My feet fell asleep in the band room and every time I stood up, I fell down!

I found some stones in my bathing suit. I pulled it down in plain sight to get the stones out – and then I came to my senses when I found my swimming trunks down by my knees.

Once I put a can of Coke in the freezer thinking it was the refrigerator. The Coke blew up all over everything.

One time I was leaning back on a chair with one foot under the TV. I leaned back too far and the TV went through the wall in our basement.

My dad and I always punch each other softly. I went up to this guy who looked like my dad and I started punching him in the stomach. Luckily, just softly.

One day I was running away from the lawn sprinkler so I wouldn't get wet and I ran right into my little brother's wading pool!!

My brother put pancakes in the microwave, but rather than cook them for two minutes, he pressed an extra zero. They blew up. (So did my mom.)

My Greatest Mistake

Name: _____

Here's the mistake I made: _____

_____

_____

Here's what I learned: _____

_____

_____

This mistake actually turned out okay when:

_____

_____

_____

_____

_____

_____

_____

_____

_____

_____

Major League Mistakes

Even the most successful people make mistakes. When they do, there is almost always something to be learned from the mistake. Here are just a few examples:

The greatest quarterbacks complete only 60% of their passes. The best basketball players make only about 50% of their shots. Most major league baseball players get on base only about 25% of the time.

What do you think these major leaguers have learned from their "mistakes"?

Top oil companies, even with the help of expert geologists, must dig an average of 10 wells before finding oil.

What do you think the geologists and other experts have learned from their "mistakes"?

Producers at the first television station that hired Oprah Winfrey tried to give her a makeover and turn her into a "talking head" reporter. It didn't work: Oprah didn't fit the station's news-anchor mold – and she didn't want to. But the station had a contract that said Winfrey could not be fired, so the producers assigned her to a local morning show called "People Are Talking." It was the beginning of Oprah's incredibly successful career as a talk show host.

What do you think the television producers learned from their "mistake"?

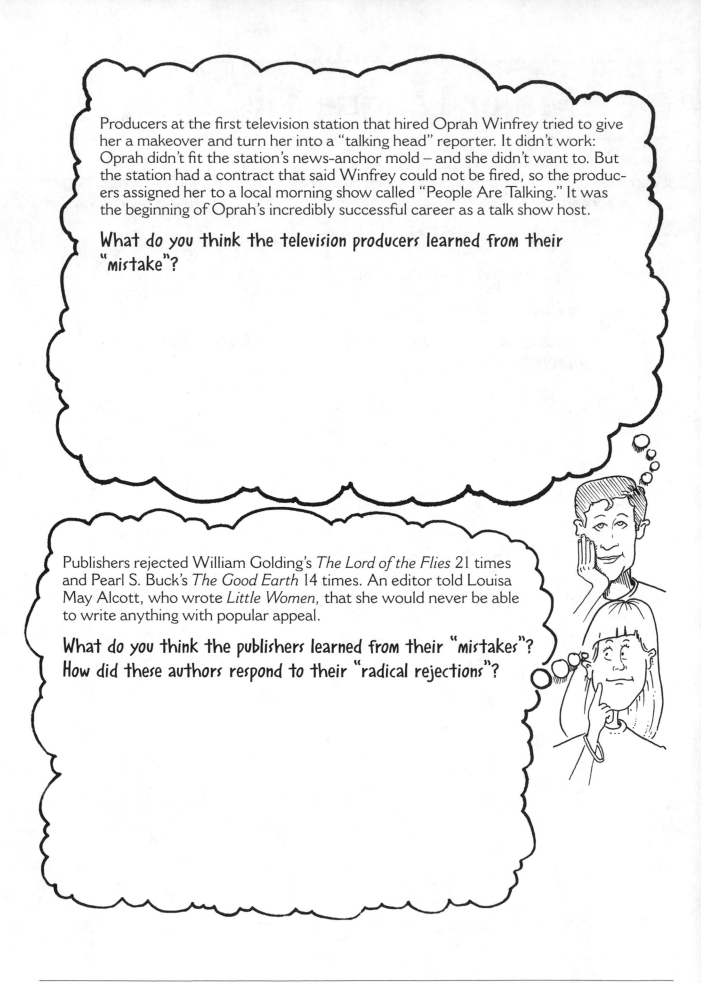

Publishers rejected William Golding's *The Lord of the Flies* 21 times and Pearl S. Buck's *The Good Earth* 14 times. An editor told Louisa May Alcott, who wrote *Little Women,* that she would never be able to write anything with popular appeal.

What do you think the publishers learned from their "mistakes"? How did these authors respond to their "radical rejections"?

I Wanna Be Bugged by You

At the beginning of the school year, many students may not be familiar with their classmates or teachers. This activity allows everyone to get to know one another a little better "from the inside out." As they write their answers to one of four questions related to important aspects of their lives, students open windows to their interests, abilities, goals, and dreams. Displayed as a centipede with many parts, students' personal stories combine to show both the diversity and the commonalities among their larger student group.

Learning Objectives

Through this activity, students will:
- identify and write about their personal strengths, interests, and goals
- identify significant people in their lives and explore why these individuals are important
- think critically and creatively
- review and ask questions about their peers' work

Product

Large, wall-size centipede with individual body segments containing students' personal stories

Related Curriculum

Language Arts, Social Studies, Art

Materials

- overhead projector and transparencies made from "Bug Myself" and "A Sampling of Bug Parts" reproducible masters (pages 27–29) *or* copies for each student

- colored construction paper (a different color for each homeroom if done with a team of classrooms)
- scissors
- crayons, markers, or paints
- paste, glue, or tape

For Classroom Extension: materials for making a large "bug head": large posterboard; Styrofoam balls (cut in half) for the eyes; glitter and glue for the nose, mouth, and rosy cheeks; pipe cleaners for antennas and eyelashes

Time

One 45-minute session

Activity Steps

1. Introduce the activity. Ask students if they know what it means to "bug" someone. Confirm that it means to pester or bother the person. Then say: "Sometimes we might 'bug' someone in a friendly way. That's what we'll do today: We'll 'bug' each other just enough to learn a little more about everyone in our class."

Tell students that they are going to write about themselves and then share what they've written, first with another student and then with the whole class.

Display or distribute copies of "Bug Myself." Read it with students and explain that they are to choose one of the situations to write about.

2. Share others' stories. Take a few minutes to offer your own take on one of the four situations or, if you team teach, ask a teammate to respond orally to one.

Then display or distribute copies of "A Sampling of Bug Parts." Read the entries together, briefly discussing what readers learn from the writers' ideas.

3. Write drafts. Allow 10–15 minutes for students to draft their responses.

4. Form "bug" pairs. Have each student pair up with another in the classroom. Ask partners to read one another's responses and "bug" each other by asking questions to help clarify or elaborate on ideas. After a few minutes of discussion, have students work individually again to refine their responses.

5. Create bug parts. After each student has written an acceptable second (or third) draft, pass out single sheets of colored construction paper and have students write their final drafts. (If you are using the activity with more than one classroom, use a different color of construction paper for each room.) Suggest that students round off the corners of the sheet so that the shape is more oval, like a centipede's body segment. Or, you may decide to let your class's centipede take a changing shape dependent on students' different writing formats.

When they finish writing, give students additional construction paper and invite them to add feet of their own unique design to their centipede part, placing their first names on one foot and their last names on the other. Students may also wish to decorate their bug parts and feet further.

6. Create and display the bug. Hang the written "bug parts" on a large wall, connected to approximate the form of a centipede. Inevitably, students will soon call this bug by some name they've invented!

For Surefire Success

Introducing this activity by telling your own story will heighten your students' interest. Many students will be eager to learn about what you might have been instead of a teacher, or whom you would invite to dinner if you could invite anyone at all. An added bonus is that students see that they can choose to answer seriously, rather than jokingly, if they wish.

Classroom Extensions

- Ask for volunteers to create a large "bug head" to lead the parade of bug body parts. The ones we create are usually made from large posterboard, using Styrofoam balls (cut in half) for the eyes; glitter and glue for the nose, mouth, and rosy cheeks; and pipe cleaners for antennas and eyelashes.

- Keep the bug's head displayed all year, but ask students to create different body parts in response to different prompts. For example: "If you could live in the past, present, or future, which would you choose and why?" "The President (Prime Minister) has asked you to lead a special commission on school improvement. What are some of the topics you'd like to address?"

Family Extension

Complete this activity during the first few weeks of school, making sure it is available for view during open house. This assignment is a tremendous hit with parents!

Variation

This is an excellent activity to do with large groups of students. For example, if you team teach with three other teachers, introduce the activity to all students at once. Then distribute construction paper, by color, to individual homerooms or classrooms. When the single large bug is posted for all to see, mix the colors; students can then read and identify their teammates' responses by homeroom or classroom.

Bug Myself

Name: _____

Read the four "buggy ideas." Then choose and write about one of the ideas:

You are allowed to invite three people, living or dead, to your home for dinner. These might be famous people; they might also be people from your personal family history. By writing about whom you will invite and why you will invite them, you'll be telling us something about the kinds of things and people you enjoy.

You have been granted three wishes: one for you, one for your family, and one for the earth. By revealing your three wishes and why they are important to you, you'll be telling us about what you value most for yourself and others.

You are about to turn 100 years old and are writing your life's story. It might even be turned into a movie! By writing about what you have done in your life, you'll be telling us about your goals and dreams.

Someone has decided to hire you for a job. Describe for us what the job is and why you are perfectly suited to do it. In this way, you'll tell us about your strengths and your interests.

A Sampling of Bug Parts

Read what some "bugged" fourth-grade students wrote about themselves:

If someone hired me to do a job I would choose to be a chemist because I love math and science, and I'm really good at them. I also like mixing and making new things. This job would also be good for me because I'm not afraid to make mistakes. If I would make a mistake, I would just keep trying until I got things right, and if I still couldn't get things right, I would ask for help. The last reason I would like to be a chemist is because I think they make a lot of money, don't they?

If I had to invite three people to dinner I would invite my mother because she died when I was five and I would like to meet her again. I would also invite Cindy Crawford because I would like to meet a famous supermodel. And last but not least I would invite Jim Carrey, because I would like to meet a funny comedian with a big mouth.

If I could invite anyone to eat dinner with me, living or dead, I would invite my real grandma, because she died before I was born. Everyone tells me that I look just like her when I don't even know who she is.

I would also invite my third-grade teacher, Miss Heflin, because she retired during the school year because of a heart problem.

Lastly, I'd invite my new cousin, Eric James, because I would like to get to know him as if he were my brother. The reason I chose him was that I only have one other cousin, and he is not allowed to do any-thing that will get him hyper. So, I'd like to have another cousin to play football and games with (I'm an only child).

Now that I'm 100 years old, here's what I've done with my life. I became a best-selling author because I love to write and I didn't have to work at it 24 hours a day, only when I had an idea. This still gave me time for my kids. When I wasn't writing or watching my kids, I trained my pets and other people's pets. All these things kept me so busy that I didn't have time to cook dinner or do the laundry, so my husband had to do those things. I retired when I was 70, moved in with my youngest child, and played with his or her children all day.

ABCs of Our Lives

All students are familiar with alphabet books, though many may think of them as books for very young children. Challenge this concept by inviting your students to research their personal histories, think introspectively, and fashion their discoveries into autobiographies in an ABC format.

For student wordsmiths, graphic designers, and visual artists alike, this is a stimulating activity that affords both self-exploration and self-expression. It also offers an opportunity for children to reminisce with their families about important events and people in their lives.

Learning Objectives

Through this activity, students will:

- identify significant people and events in their lives
- plan and carry out a project over several days
- write creatively within an assigned framework
- review and edit their peers' work

Product

Individual, student-created alphabet books

Related Curriculum

Language Arts, Social Studies, Art

Materials

- several ABC books
- materials for making books (see "Four Ways to Make a Book," pages 33–36)
- copies of "Alphabetical Me" handout (pages 37–39) for each student

- overhead projector and transparency made from "The ABCs of Editing" reproducible master (pages 40–41) or copies for each student
- dictionaries and thesauruses
- colored pencils, pens, crayons, or markers for writing and decorating final copies

Optional: cassette player and cassette of soft background music

Time

One 40-minute session to introduce the activity; additional at-home and in-school time to complete it

Preparation

Select one or two alphabet books to serve as an introduction to the entire lesson. Consider one of your personal favorites; your own excitement about the book will inspire your students to become actively involved in this activity. If possible, select additional books for students to look at as well. Try to find examples that are designed, written, and illustrated in a variety of ways. For example, some books rely on illustrations while others use single words or paragraphs to get their messages across. Plan to keep these books in the classroom so that students may look at them during the course of the activity.

Read "Four Ways to Make a Book." Determine what types of book-making options you wish to have available for your students. Assemble the materials specified for these types of books.

Activity Steps

1. Introduce the activity. Before showing any books, ask students to share their own ideas about alphabet books. You might ask questions such as:

- What do alphabet books try to do?
- How do the words and art communicate messages to the reader?
- Do you have a favorite alphabet book? Why do you like it so much?

2. Share favorite ABC books. Following this initial discussion, read one or two of your favorite ABC books with the students. Provide specific details about what it is that you like about the books. You might also wish to share a few other books by providing a very brief overview of each one. Point out that alphabet books might do one of several things, including:

- focus on one main idea or topic
- incorporate a rhythmic pattern (such as alliteration or rhyme)
- rely heavily on illustrations to get the main idea across to the reader.

The main goal during this initial contact with alphabet books is to have the students recognize the power that these books have to convey specific messages.

Tell students that they will be looking at and discussing other alphabet books in preparation for creating their own personal books.

3. Explore ideas in small groups. Depending upon the number of books you have, divide the class into groups of 2–4 students to examine one or two alphabet books. Allow about 10 minutes for students to review the books and identify:

- the way the authors have used the alphabet
- the element of the book that the group likes the most (such as illustration, rhyming verse, alliteration).

4. Share ideas in the large group. Have one person from each group describe the group's books and the primary method the authors used to get their ideas across to the reader. Be sure to highlight instances in which the authors used words and phrases effectively to "paint a picture" for the readers.

5. Plan and write ABC statements. Challenge students to describe their life in an alphabet format. Distribute copies of the "Alphabetical Me" handout and review the directions together.

It is important that students understand how to develop each of the letters for their alphabet book. Ask them to construct thoughts for each letter that can be elaborated through words or pictures. Explain that they will not merely describe themselves. Point out how this is done in other ABC books. Be sure to remind students to capture the important events, people, and places in their lives. You might give examples such as:

- **B** is for the **B**each – any **B**each. I just love the salt air and water.
- **T** is for **T**he **T**rain I ride **T**o school with my mom, who rides **T**o work.
- **L** is for **L**ove: for **L**aughter, **L**ong walks, **L**ullabies, **L**itter cleanup, the **L**ibrary, and **L**unch. These are all things I enjoy with the people I **L**ove.

Allow time both in the classroom and at home for students to complete this activity. Encourage students to talk to other students who know them well. Family members might also be great sources of ideas and inspiration. Remind students to use the dictionary and thesaurus to help them find words for their ideas.

6. Confer with students as needed. Throughout the process of creating ABC books, you will need to confer with students individually to be sure that they have a grasp on the format and on your expectations. Often, students might need a specific suggestion for a letter or an idea that doesn't seem to take shape. The following might be helpful:

- It will be natural for students to shape each letter into a very simple thought, such as: "A is for Ann, my middle name." Encourage children to expand upon a simple phrase: "A is for Ann, my middle name – a name my grandmother gave me."

- Suggest that students jump around from letter to letter, working first with those letters for which an idea comes quickly.

- Help students see ways to reshape ideas to fit certain letters. For example, if a student has already used the word "math" to go with the letter M, suggest for S: "S is for school, a place where I really enjoy math class."

- Encourage students to be creative about using letters such as X and Z: "X is part of tic-tac-toe, which my uncle and I play while I wait for my allergy shot." "X is the railroad X-ing I X every day on the bus." "Z is an N turned NiNety degreeZ, which is the temperature I like best!"

7. Have peers review and edit the ABC statements. As the activity takes shape and students seem to have a majority of their letters and statements completed, have the students pair up with others in the classroom. Ask pairs to consult with each other, offering both positive feedback and constructive criticism. Display or distribute copies of "The ABCs of Editing" and explain that partners are to use the ideas presented to guide them as they review one another's writing.

This will help students edit and refine their ideas. It will also allow them to explore ideas about those letters for which inspiration still eludes them. Through this peer review process, students will learn that creativity and problem solving benefit from collaboration with others.

8. Create ABC books. This is the step in which students turn their statements into books. It may be helpful for you to present a few specific ideas for the students so that they won't become blocked as they decide upon a format. For example, some students may feel that a picture book will work best, while others may like to design a fold-out poster book or a flip book.

Once the students have determined a format for their work, have them proceed with their final copies. Because students have worked so hard up to this point, stress that they should take the time to really show off their ideas in a creative and colorful way.

If you like, put on some music in the background and circulate among the students to encourage them as they work.

Classroom Extension

Once the books are bound, have an alphabet book reading party so that students have an opportunity to share their books and to read those of their peers. You might also wish to arrange for the books to be displayed in the media center, or send some to the principal to read.

Family Extension

Plan an alphabet book reading party for families. Include punch and cookies along with the readings to give the party the flavor of a library or bookstore event. Design or have students design their own "business cards" (as authors, poets, artists, or designers) to pass out during the reading party.

Four Ways to Make a Book

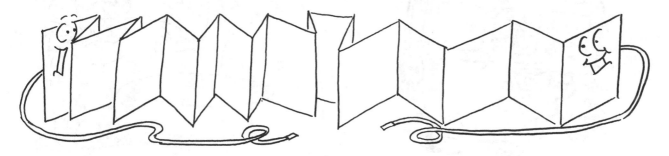

I. Fold-Out Book

HERE'S WHAT YOU NEED:

- several sheets of construction paper of equal sizes
- tape
- yarn

HERE'S WHAT YOU DO:

1. Arrange the pages in a row.

2. Tape the pages together and fold them accordion-style.

3. Unfold the pages and tape yarn to the back of the opened book. To close the book, fold it again and tie the yarn in front.

SUGGESTIONS:

- Make a group book for which each person contributes a page.
- Make a wordless picture book.
- Make pocket pages: Cut sheets of construction paper in half. Tape the half-sheets to each page, leaving the top open to form a pocket. Use the pockets to hold quarter-page sheets that tell or expand on the story of the large page.

II. Shape Book

HERE'S WHAT YOU NEED:

- construction paper for the book's cover
- plain or lined paper for the book's pages
- paper punch and yarn *or* stapler
- scissors

HERE'S WHAT YOU DO:

1. Place sheets of plain or lined paper between two pieces of construction paper.

2. Sew or staple the book together along the left-hand side.

3. On the book's front cover, draw an outline of the desired shape. The sewn or stapled book edge should stay within the outline.

4. Cut along the outline, making sure the binding remains intact.

SUGGESTIONS:

- Use a shape that represents the subject of the book.
- Ask students to predict from the shape what the book will be about.

III. Softcover Book

HERE'S WHAT YOU NEED:

- sheets (8½" x 11") of plain paper (using both sides of the paper, one sheet makes eight book pages)
- needle and thread
- scissors or butter knife
- construction paper, wallpaper, or cloth for the book's cover
- glue

HERE'S WHAT YOU DO:

1. Stack the sheets of plain paper evenly and fold them in half. Fold them in half a second time.

2. With needle and thread, sew the pages along the second fold. To do this, start at the middle of the folded edge and stitch up to the top edge; then stitch all the way down to the bottom edge; then stitch back up to the middle. Tie off the thread ends.

3. Use a scissors or butter knife to slit the remaining folded page edges.

4. Cut the paper or cloth for the cover so its size is 5½" x 8½". Glue the cover to the front and back facing pages.

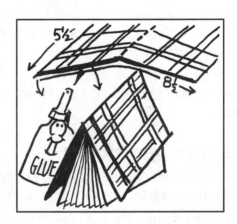

IV. Hardcover Book

HERE'S WHAT YOU NEED:

- sheets (8½" x 11") of plain paper (using both sides of the paper, one sheet makes four book pages)
- needle and thread
- wallpaper or wrapping paper for cover
- two sheets (at least 9½" x 6½") cardboard, such as shirt cardboard
- glue
- two sheets (8½" x 5⅜") construction paper

HERE'S WHAT YOU DO:

1. Stack the sheets of plain paper evenly and fold them in half.

2. With needle and thread, sew the pages along the fold, ⅛" from the folded edge. (If you wish, you can use a sewing machine to stitch the pages. This is a good technique if you want to mass-produce the books.)

3. Cut wallpaper or wrapping paper about two inches larger than the open book on all sides.

4. Cut each sheet of cardboard a little larger than a single book page. Place the cardboard sheets on the wrong side of the wallpaper or wrapping paper, leaving a ¼" space for the book's spine. Glue and fold the

corners and edges of the cover to the cardboard, as shown.

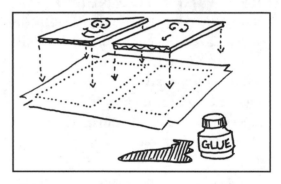

5. Glue the front facing page, spine, and back facing page to the cardboard side (inside) of the cover, as shown.

6. Glue construction paper to inside front and back covers.

7. Close the book to ensure proper folding. Let it dry.

Alphabetical Me

Use the alphabet to describe and explain different things about yourself. You will need to think creatively and carefully about the important people and events in your life.

Using just a word or two is not enough. You need to use phrases that describe and explain what it is about yourself that you want your reader to understand.

Once you have completed and edited your alphabet, you will use what you have written to create your own personal ABC book.

A FEW REMINDERS...

✔ Be sure that each entry relates directly to you!

✔ Be careful in selecting words:

Example: **B** is for Brian, <u>that</u> is my oldest brother.
("That" is incorrect; "who" is correct.)

✔ Be sure you have included descriptive details:

Not enough detail: **A** is for athletics...a fun thing.
(This does not tell anything about you.)

M is for movies, which I love.
(This does not tell enough about you.)

C is for Carla, my oldest sister.
(This does not tell why Carla is important to you.)

Good detail: **A** is for athletics, which I enjoy. Basketball is my favorite sport.

M is for movies, which I love – all kinds, but especially scary ones.

C is for Carla, my oldest sister, who loves tennis and always helps me with my homework.

My ABC Book

Name: _____

A
B
C
D
E
F
G
H
I
J
K

L
M
N
O
P
Q
R
S
T
U
V
W
X
Y
Z

The ABCs of Editing

By yourself...

A. Reread your entries. Place an asterisk **(*)** next to three statements that you really <u>love</u>. These are the ones of which you are the most proud.

B. Place a question mark **(?)** next to those letters that still need statements or, in your opinion, need better or different statements.

C. Place a dash **(–)** next to three items that you will agree to change.

With your partner...

D. Exchange papers and read each other's ABCs without making any comments or asking any questions.

E. Discuss the entries together. Ask questions if an entry is not clear to you. Offer praise for statements that you really like.

F. Reread the items in your partner's paper that have a question mark **(?)** or dash **(–)** next to them. Write down any ideas you have that might help the writer edit these statements. Can you suggest details or words that will make the entry more interesting? More moving? More fun?

By yourself...

G. Take back your ABC statements from your partner. Look again at those entries you have marked with a dash **(–)**. Concentrate on re-working these entries so that the language "sparkles."

H. Go back to the items highlighted with a question mark **(?)**. Read the suggestions your partner wrote and make any changes you think will improve your statements.

With your partner...

I. Share your rewritten statements.

J. Work together to help each other finalize all the entries.

By yourself...

K. Put the "finishing touches" on your writing!

Little Stories of Our Classroom

 ithin your classroom walls there are hundreds of stories waiting to be told. Here's an opportunity to give voice to some of those stories. As students write and share their personal ideas and experiences, they gain an appreciation for the special characteristics that make up the personalities in their classroom. They also recognize that their diverse traits and histories combine into a cohesive unit with its own unique collective personality. The resulting class biography is an excellent project to complete before an open house or parent conferences. The completed books are well received by parents.

Learning Objectives

Through this activity, students will:

- identify similarities and differences among students in the class
- recognize that there is more to people than what we see on the surface
- tell their personal stories orally
- interview one another and write one another's personal stories
- review and edit their peers' writing

Product

Class book that includes the writings and drawings of the participating students

Related Curriculum

Language Arts, Social Studies, Art

Materials

- copies of "The Me I'd Like Others to See" and "I'd Like to Get to Know You" handouts (pages 45–47) for each student

- materials for making books (see "Four Ways to Make a Book," pages 33–36)
- dictionaries and thesauruses
- pens, crayons, or markers for illustrating the stories

For Classroom Extension: camera and film

For Variations: opaque projector, black and white construction paper, index cards, tape or glue; cassette recorder and blank cassettes

Time

Two 40-minute sessions; additional in-school time to assemble the class book

Activity Steps

1. Introduce the activity. Explain to students that they will be working together to write a classroom "history" book: a compilation of brief stories about everyone in the classroom. Instead of writing about themselves, students will interview and write about each other.

2. Discuss similarities and differences. On the chalkboard, draw a line and make two columns, titled "Same" and "Different." Ask students to look around the room at their classmates and share specific characteristics that make them similar (for example, all attend the same school) as well as those that make them different (for example, gender or hair color). List these in their respective columns.

3. Share some things others don't yet know. Distribute copies of the "The Me I'd Like Others to See" handout. Review the questions together and ask students to complete the handout while you do the same.

For item 2, help students understand that they are to describe a specific characteristic or trait about themselves. For item 5, explain that students are to write a specific piece of information about themselves that they believe is important for others to know.

After approximately five minutes, share with students the "secrets" you have written about yourself. Ask for volunteers to share their ideas also.

4. Talk about assumptions. Discuss how people form opinions and ideas about others. You might ask questions such as:

- Why do we assume things about people?
- Why don't we always know what a person is really like?
- Why is it worthwhile to learn more about people? What are some ways to do this?

Make the point that sometimes we don't take the time to find out what a person is really like. Many times, we only think about people in terms of what is most obvious about them: actions, behaviors, even the clothes they wear. Then ask:

- What makes us a special class?

Continue with a discussion centering on the notion that it is the group's collective similarities and differences that make the class unique.

5. Conduct interviews. Explain that students will work in pairs and will share more about the ideas they wrote on the "The Me I'd Like Others to See" handout. Distribute the "I'd Like to Get to Know You" handout. Review it with students, explaining that partners can use this sheet as they interview one another. Encourage partners to ask their own questions about the responses, too, to gather additional information about each other. Interviewers may want to focus on only one or two ideas or ask questions about all of the ideas. Make sure students understand that they will use the information they acquire to write about their partner.

Give an example for item 2, such as being musical. A musical person may come from a family of musicians or may be the only one in the family who enjoys music. The person may like to listen to music, play it, sing it, dance to it, or write it.

He or she may take lessons or give lessons to other people.

Then have students pair up and get to work learning about their partners. Allow 10–15 minutes for this step of the activity. Remind students of the time remaining halfway through and again when there are approximately three minutes remaining.

6. Write stories. Have students write independently about the people they interviewed. Before they begin, share a few of the following "little stories" written by our fifth-grade students. Focus attention on how the stories are written: They are specifically about the unique characteristics of each individual, they are brief, and they are to the point.

- Jeannette is a French girl filled with forgiveness and kindness. She is very generous and smart, and her smile makes you happy. She'll never turn you down no matter what happens.
- Patrick is the hilarious type, always making you happy when you're gloomy and happier when you're already in a good mood. Patrick is smart, a good actor, but best of all, my friend.
- Elena is a smiley person. She laughs, giggles, and acts as if she's having a ball. In academics she's under control and doesn't know the meaning of "upset."
- Maruf is a good cartoonist – he makes them up! He is very smart and a whiz at the computer. I like him a lot. He makes me happy.

Have students use the information obtained during their interviews to construct their pieces of writing. You might wish to specify the number of sentences.

7. Have peers review and edit the stories. Have students divide into pairs, this time with a different partner. Explain that these pairs will act as peer editors to help revise one another's writing. Encourage students to help with the selection of words, in particular, so that the writing really "paints a picture" for the reader. Remind them to use a thesaurus to diversify their word choice and the dictionary to check spelling and word meanings.

8. Share stories. Once the revisions are completed, have students meet with their original partners. Students are to read the stories about themselves and let the writers know if the information is accurate. Allow time for students to work individually to put the finishing touches on their stories.

9. Complete the class book. Once the stories are written in final form, decide together how to compile them into a book by discussing questions such as these:

- Will we write the stories by hand or type them on the computer?
- What size paper will we use?
- How many stories will go on each page?
- How will we illustrate the book?

One idea is to ask for volunteers to draw caricatures of students. This is a wonderful opportunity for budding artists!

Classroom Extension

Following the completion of the writing, consider designing a bulletin board or hallway display that includes photos of the students next to the short stories about them.

School Extension

Send students to interview and write about other people in the school: the principal, secretary, custodian, teachers, other students.

Family Extensions

- Have students interview and write about members of their family.
- Suggest that students work with members of their families to create family books for which members interview and write about one another.

Variations

- Create a bulletin board display that uses silhouettes of the students' heads (made using an opaque projector) with the stories written on index cards and taped or glued on the silhouettes.
- Have students prepare brief oral presentations about the people they interviewed. Record the presentations and combine them into a class audiobook.

The Me I'd Like Others to See

Name: _____

There are many things about each of us that others do not know. Some things we want to keep to ourselves. There are other things about us, though, that we'd really like others in the class to know. Think about some things you'd like your classmates to know about you. Write your ideas:

1. Most people don't know that I am very interested in: _____

_____

_____

2. Most people don't know this about me: _____

_____

_____

3. Most people don't know that a hobby I enjoy is: _____

_____

_____

4. Three words to describe me are: _____

_____

_____

5. The one thing I would like everyone to know about me is: _____

_____

_____

I'd Like to Get to Know You

My name: _____

Name of student I interviewed: _____

Use the questions on this sheet to help you learn more about your partner. If you think of other questions to ask, that's great!

1. What is something that really interests you?
Why does it interest you?
How did you learn about it?
Is someone else interested in it, too? Who?
What have you learned about it?

_____
_____
_____
_____

2. What is a unique trait you have?
What is something about you that's very special?
How did you discover that about yourself?
Does someone else you know have the same trait?
How do you use the trait? Where? When?
Why are you glad you have that trait?

_____
_____
_____
_____

3. What is something most people don't know about you?

Why don't they know it?

Why do you want people to know that about you?

How could I explain that some more?

_____

_____

_____

_____

_____

_____

4. What is a special hobby you enjoy?

How did you get started on your hobby?

Does someone else enjoy the hobby with you? Who?

Why do you enjoy it so much?

When do you do your hobby?

How much time do you spend on it?

What have you had to do to learn more about your hobby?

_____

_____

_____

_____

_____

_____

_____

Box Up Your Life

We often ask students to write autobiographically or to draw or paint self-portraits. In this activity, students work on a different kind of self-portrait, a symbolic one. First, students think about the aspects of themselves and their lives that are most important to them. Then they look for objects that symbolize each aspect. Finally, students assemble the objects into a boxed display representative of themselves. You and your students will marvel at the variety of both interests and expression this project inspires.

Learning Objectives

Through this activity, students will:

- identify personal characteristics, preferences, interests, feelings, and beliefs
- recognize commonalities among themselves
- think and work creatively to craft a personalized display box
- symbolize both abstract and concrete ideas

Product

Individual, student-created "life boxes"

Related Curriculum

Language Arts, Social Studies, Math, Art

Materials

- copies of "A Plan to Box Up My Life" handout (pages 50–51) for each student
- shoe box for each student
- art materials for creating and decorating boxes (foam core, cardboard, glue, paints, wrapping paper, and so on)

Optional: Wilfrid Gordon McDonald Partridge by Mem Fox

For Family Extension: camcorder and blank videocassette

Time

One 45-minute session to introduce the activity; additional at-home or in-class time to complete the boxes; five minutes per student for presentation of boxes

Preparation

This activity seems to work best when the teacher also shares a life box. Create yours ahead of time to share with students when you introduce the activity. Include a variety of aspects of yourself: physical traits that describe you, interests or hobbies, important beliefs, pivotal experiences, goals.

Activity Steps

1. Introduce the activity. Ask the class how they would describe the idea of "memory" to a creature from another planet who does not know the meaning of the word. Encourage students to respond in different directions by asking such questions as:

- What picture comes to your mind when you hear the word "memory"?
- What color do you think "memory" is? Why?
- If you used one object to demonstrate a special memory you have, what would it be? Why?

Optional: If you have a copy of *Wilfrid Gordon McDonald Partridge*, share this heartwarming story with your students. It introduces the art of describing an abstract trait, such as memory, in concrete terms. Read the story to the class and follow it with a discussion about Wilfrid Gordon's attempts to get Miss Nancy's memory back for her. Review the words used in the book to describe memory.

2. Discuss ways to visually represent abstract concepts. Ask students to think about some ways to "show" abstract concepts. Ask questions similar to these:

- What does "friendship" ("peace," "love") mean to you?
- What object could you use to show the concept of friendship (peace, love)?

Show students your life box and review how it uses objects to represent some of your memories as well as other characteristics about you. Explain to students that they will be using this idea of representing characteristics with objects in a creative project about their own lives. As you share your box, be specific about why you selected certain items and why you decorated your box as you did.

3. Do personal brainstorming. Give students copies of the "A Plan to Box Up My Life" handout and have them independently brainstorm 15 characteristics, interests, feelings, beliefs, preferences, goals, or other things that make up what's most important in their lives. Be sure they include at least three abstract concepts such as feelings, shared values, or personal traits. Here are a few starter ideas:

- *feelings:* love, excitement, confusion, joy, trust, hope, anticipation, closeness
- *shared values:* religious faith, interest in politics, care for the environment, love of family
- *personal traits:* musical, athletic, thoughtful, clever, different, jumpy
- *hobbies and interests:* photography, collecting baseball cards, pets, skating, music

Next to each item, students should write down a specific object or thing they could use to represent that aspect of themselves.

After brainstorming, have students mark with an asterisk (*) the 10 aspects that they consider to be the most creative and unique and that best

represent them. Be sure that students now include at least two abstract concepts.

4. Explain how to make the boxes. Encourage students to use their own ideas for both filling and decorating their life boxes. Offer these guidelines:

- Include in your box at least 10 items that symbolize your most significant interests and personal characteristics.
- Plan and construct your box carefully so it's a complete and well-designed self-portrait.
- Decorate your box in a way that reflects something about yourself. (For example, cover it in wrapping paper with a balloon design to represent your love of celebrations.)

Give a specific date when you want the life boxes to be completed and brought into class. Offer both an oral and a written reminder on the board at least two days before the boxes are due.

5. Share the boxes in class. It is best to space these presentations so that everyone is attentive during the descriptions. We have found that three or four at one time seem to keep everyone's attention.

For Surefire Success

Before starting this activity, be sure you have collected enough boxes. You may wish to have each student bring in a box by a certain date. One good source of boxes is a discount shoe store that doesn't rely on shoe boxes being distributed with their product.

School Extension

Explain your project to your principal, another school administrator, another teacher, or other school personnel. Ask these individuals to prepare their own life boxes to share as a surprise to your students.

Family Extension

Videotape the presentations. Then loan the video to families (for a weekend or a few days) or play it at the beginning of an open house or in a common waiting area during conferences.

A Plan to Box Up My Life

Name: _____

Use these categories to get started brainstorming. Add as many others as you wish!

My feelings:

My interests:

My hobbies:

Things I like:

My favorite possessions:

My beliefs:

Values I share with someone else:

My special traits:

People who are important to me:

My goals:

Other ideas about myself:

Personal Classroom Pledge

What better way to build community than by allowing students to cooperatively fashion a set of principles upon which they want their classroom to operate? In this activity, students take center stage, working first in small groups and then the larger group to identify and agree on common classroom and personal goals. As you guide your students through this activity, you will foster teamwork, responsibility, and personal growth. At the same time, you will give your students hands-on experience in the democratic process.

Though the inspiration for this activity came from the U.S. Pledge of Allegiance, the activity is universal to democratic classrooms everywhere. Your "personal classroom pledge" can be the centerpiece for discussions of citizenship and democracy.

Learning Objectives

Through this activity, students will:

- work and think cooperatively toward a common goal
- discuss and resolve issues related to classroom design
- understand the need for personal and social commitments
- experience a cooperative way to arrive at consensus

Product

Group-created classroom pledge

Materials

- copies of "Planning Our Pledge" handout (pages 55–56) for each student
- overhead projector and transparency made from "A Fifth-Grade Classroom Pledge" reproducible master (page 57) or copies for each group of 4–5 students
- newsprint or flipchart
- marker
- dictionary
- unlined 8½" x 11" or 8½" x 14" paper (you will type the finished pledge on one sheet and make a copy for each student)
- one large sheet of posterboard

Optional: parchment paper and ribbon, *or* laminating material

Time

Two 45-minute sessions

Background

The genesis for this lesson occurred in Jim's classroom one mid-November day. As the students were preparing to open another day of class, they stood to make a rote recitation of the Pledge of Allegiance. Like millions of their school-age counterparts across the U.S., the students droned on, looking at the ceiling, their friends, or blank space.

Jim had had it. "Stop!" he commanded in a voice not quite loud enough to be considered a shout, but with enough volume to put the kibosh on the morning's pledge.

"You can't stop us!" cried a shocked Michael. "It's the Pledge of Allegiance!"

At this point, Jim had the students sit down and do two things: Define the words "pledge" and "allegiance" and write the Pledge of Allegiance from start to finish.

The results, if nothing else, were informative and humorous. Every student (these were fourth graders) mixed up at least one line in the pledge; only one student even came close to deciphering the word "indivisible." The humor came in the form of a P.S. from Rachel, who informed Jim that, until third grade, she thought the first line of the pledge was "I led the pigeons to the flag." Since Rachel knew neither the word "pledge" nor "allegiance," it made perfect sense to her to parade pigeons to the Stars and Stripes!

It was at this point that we began having our students write their own classroom pledge. After all, we reasoned, if the students didn't understand the meaning behind a morning ritual they had been enacting for four years, then we needed to begin with a more basic lesson. Here it is:

Activity Steps

1. Introduce the activity. Divide students into working groups of 4–5 students. Ask them to think of several things that all of them agree to this year in relation to:

- school and schoolwork
- friendships
- families
- personal values
- the earth and the environment
- anything else important to them that doesn't fall under one of the first five categories.

2. Discuss and write pledges in small groups. Display or distribute to the groups "A Fifth-Grade Classroom Pledge"; give all students a copy of the "Planning Our Pledge" handout. Ask the groups to begin writing each section of their personal classroom pledge with the words "I promise" followed by the commitments agreed upon by everyone in their group.

Tell the students to keep their individual promises short (no more than 20 lines for the total pledge). Encourage them to use the example of the fifth-grade pledge to stimulate their own ideas. As you mingle with each cooperative working group, help students to edit their thoughts and language into the simplest of terms.

3. Discuss pledges with the whole class. Invite one member of each group to read the section on school and schoolwork. At the end of each group's recitation, ask the class: "Is there anyone in the class who cannot promise something that was just read?" If a student cites a specific objection, ask him or her to elaborate on why the statement is not acceptable. Ask the student or others in the class whether different wording would resolve the problem. If after several minutes of discussion you are not able to reach a compromise, drop the idea (at least for now) and move on to the next statement. For each group's statements, write on the newsprint the general ideas or specific words upon which everyone agrees.

Continue this process through each of the six categories, allowing a different group to go first each time. Again, write down only those promises that all students say they can keep.

4. Edit the pledge. Ask each group to elect one member of their initial work group to help complete the final editing of the classroom pledge. Allow this group of editors to take the newsprint notes and go off alone to compose a final draft of the ideas everyone has agreed to. Tell the group to edit or rewrite on the newsprint pages and prepare a clean copy of the edited pledge on fresh newsprint sheets. Remind the group to use the dictionary to verify spellings.

When the editors return, have them address the class with their revamped classroom pledge, making minor modifications as suggested by students.

5. Finalize the pledge. When everyone has approved the final form of the pledge, type it on the upper two-thirds of a sheet of 8½" x 11" or 8½" x 14" paper, leaving room for each student's signature at the bottom. Post the pledge and give a photocopy to each student. Also, copy the pledge (or ask a student to copy it) onto posterboard to display in your classroom.

6. Recite the pledge. Every morning after reciting the Pledge of Allegiance, join students in reciting their own personal classroom pledge.

For Surefire Success

For an added touch of importance, copy this original pledge onto sheets of parchment paper, tie each sheet with a ribbon, and give a copy to every student. Or laminate a copy of the pledge for each student's personal use.

Classroom Extension

Ask students which parts of this activity were the most difficult. Odds are, it will be the disagreements that arose in trying to arrive at language and ideas everyone could agree with. Use this as a springboard for a discussion of the difficulties family, community, and business groups face every day, even on ideas for which there is general agreement. The difficulty – at home, in social groups, in politics, and in our classrooms – comes in the fine details.

Variation

If the activity process seems too cumbersome, try this alternative: In a whole-class setting, ask students to name, individually, some things they can promise in each of the six categories listed in Activity Step 1. Write each individual promise on the board. After 15–20 minutes, when there are no more suggestions to be made, ask students to close their eyes while you read each statement. Say: "If you cannot make this promise because you're afraid you can't keep it, raise your hand and I'll erase that statement from the board. Only the items that are left at the end, the ones that everyone agrees to promise, will be included in our pledge."

Planning Our Pledge

Use this sheet to write notes about ideas for your classroom pledge. You may also want to use it for writing and editing your group's statements.

SCHOOL AND SCHOOLWORK

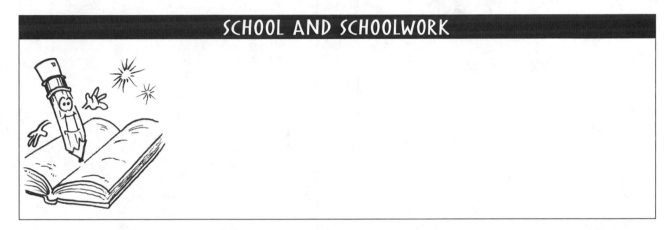

FRIENDSHIPS

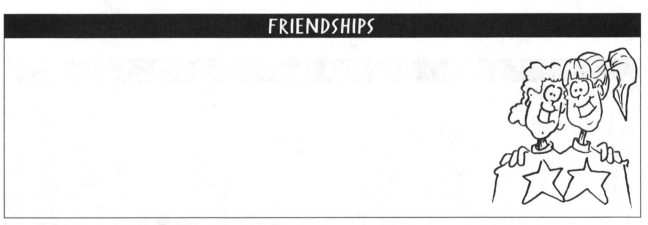

FAMILIES

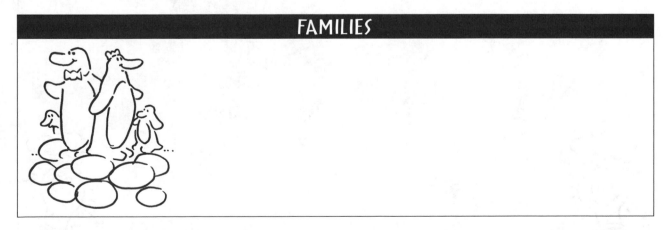

PERSONAL VALUES

THE EARTH AND THE ENVIRONMENT

OTHER IDEAS

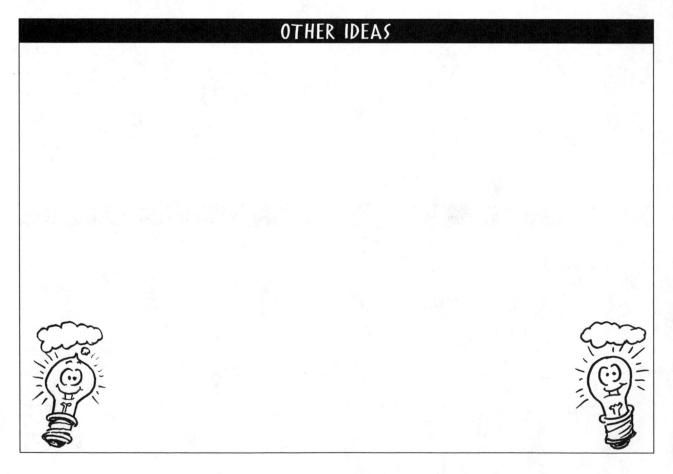

A Fifth-Grade Classroom
P L E D G E

As a member of Ms. Martinez's fifth-grade class, I promise to do all these things to the best of my ability:

1. I promise not to steal or look in other people's private things.

2. I promise I will try to be honest.

3. I promise to compliment others whenever I can.

4. I promise to be aware of the world around me by helping to recycle in my classroom.

5. I promise to keep myself and others healthy by not spreading germs.

6. I promise to try to use my imagination whenever possible.

Signed this day, October 14, by:

License to Be Me

irtually every U.S. state allows its residents to order specially designed "vanity plates" – license plates that carry personalized letters and numbers. Kids love these colorful license plates and the cryptic messages many seem to carry. Here's an activity that taps into this cultural phenomenon, inviting students to use their knowledge, creativity, and humor to craft clever and expressive vanity plates of their own.

We use this activity on the first day of school, having students write their names on the back of their plates along with an explanation of why they created their specific slogan and design. Then we hang the plates on a clothesline in the classroom. (Our teacher license plate is HERE 4 U.) Later, students can attach the plates to their tables or desks.

An added note: This activity may B EZ 4 U, but for your students it could B MY T TUF.

Good luck – and beep beep!

Learning Objectives

Through this activity, students will:

- symbolize both abstract and concrete ideas
- work creatively within a standard format
- consider their own unique traits and interests and design a license plate that displays these qualities

Product

Individual "vanity" license plates that reflect some aspect of the students, their school, their community, their nation, or their world

Related Curriculum

Language Arts, Social Studies, Art

Materials

- colored construction paper (one sheet per student)
- scissors
- crayons or markers
- other decorative art materials

For Classroom Extension: copies of "License Plates of the Rich and Famous (and Others, Too)" handout (pages 60–61) for each student

Time

One 45-minute session

Activity Steps

1. Introduce the activity. Ask students if anyone they know has a special license plate. Write the plates' letters and numbers on the board, and invite students to suggest what their messages might be.

2. Give and discuss other examples. Write some other plate messages and ask students who might own each plate. You can use ideas of your own, tapping into the interests of your students, or use some of these:

EIEIO *(a farmer, Old MacDonald)*

HIGH CS *(an opera singer, a sailor)*

1 PLUS 1 *(a kindergarten teacher)*

T 4 2 *(a tap dancer, the queen of England)*

ON R OL *(an honors student, a gambler)*

OK 2 B U *(psychologist)*

7 WE GUYZ *(the Seven Dwarfs)*

KITE KEY *(Benjamin Franklin)*

7 FT BULL *(Michael Jordan)*

EZ DUZ IT *(a tightrope walker)*

3. Talk about symbolism. Explain to students that each of these plates *symbolizes* something important to its owner. It might symbolize someone's appearance (7 WE GUYZ), personality or philosophy (OK 2 B U), accomplishments (KITE KEY), or occupation (EIEIO). Remind students that symbolic ideas may be open to a wide range of meanings and interpretations, and that this is OK.

4. Design vanity plates. By now, your students will be eager to get started designing their own vanity plates. Tell them to think of something unique about themselves: a personality trait, a goal, an activity they love, or anything that indicates who they are or what their lives are about. Ask them to follow these guidelines:

- Use any combination of letters or numbers, but no more than a total of seven. Remember that numbers can be used for words. Just think of what the number name sounds like: "1" can be "one" *or* "won"; "8" can be "eight" *or* "ate."

- Think of several ideas first before selecting the license plate that suits you best. Don't just go with your first idea – some of your later ones may be more creative. Place your best idea on a piece of construction paper about the size of a license plate. Don't forget to save room for your unique illustration. Do all of your printing and drawing in markers or crayon.

- On the back of your plate, write your name and briefly tell what message your license plate intends to send (because others may interpret the message differently).

For Surefire Success

Allow students to work in teams or with partners, if they choose. For some kids, the abstract nature of this lesson is initially difficult to decipher; talking it over with someone may help reluctant students to fully take part in the activity.

Classroom Extensions

- Have students who finish early work in small groups to complete the "License Plates of the Rich and Famous (and Others, Too)" handout. To take the activity a step further into history and literature, you may wish to have students complete the handout after, or in conjunction with, a biographical study of some of the people cited. Here are some "starter" ideas for the license plates on the handout:

Abraham Lincoln	4 SCORE
Rosa Parks	FYT 2 RYD
Lawyer	I SUE U
Computer Programmer	I BYTE
Cinderella	SLIP R
Gulliver	BIG N LTL
Boston Tea Party	NO T TAX
Leaning Tower of Pisa	ITALEAN

- Some U.S. states offer a variety of license plate designs from which to choose. (For example, some Florida plates highlight Cape Canaveral; Indiana has a plate emblazoned "Put Kids First," printed in a child's scrawl; and Connecticut's plate holds a colorful lighthouse, indicating that state's seacoast location.) Design a background for a standard license plate for your state or province. Send some of the most creative ideas to your legislators and ask them to consider the designs for adoption.

School Extension

Sponsor a schoolwide license plate contest devoted to a particular topic. Some ideas: license plates for Olympic athletes, for current-events personalities, for fictional characters.

License Plates of the Rich and Famous (and Others, Too)

Name: _____

Write a vanity plate message for one or two choices in each group:

1. Famous people in history

Thomas Jefferson   _____

Clara Barton   _____

Abraham Lincoln   _____

Susan B. Anthony   _____

Confucius   _____

Rosa Parks   _____

Juan Ponce de León   _____

Frederick Douglass   _____

Indira Gandhi   _____

2. Occupations

Blacksmith   _____

Cook   _____

Lawyer   _____

Artist   _____

Physician   _____

School principal   _____

Computer programmer   _____

3. Fictional characters and places

Bigfoot   _____

E.T.   _____

Cinderella   _____

Land of Oz   _____

Gulliver   _____

Never-Never Land   _____

4. Historical sites and events

Moon Landing   _____

Boston Tea Party   _____

Mount Rushmore   _____

The White House   _____

Leaning Tower of Pisa   _____

Taj Mahal   _____

Pyramids to the Sun and Moon   _____

Great Wall of China   _____

Celebration Streamers

Celebrations need not mark only the most momentous occasions. Along the paths we travel lie a bounty of notable smaller stops and turns – new accomplishments, heightened understandings, fresh starts, and sheer wonder! Life is full of moments worth celebrating. This activity provides an opportunity for students to gain an appreciation of these "little moments" in their lives. As they reflect upon the significance of everyday occurrences, students identify those occasions, some personal and some universal, worth noting and celebrating.

Learning Objectives

Through this activity, students will:

- identify both small and large aspects of their lives that are worth celebrating
- work cooperatively toward a common goal
- explore their own and their classmates' interests and aspirations

Product

Strips of paper identifying things worth celebrating, taped together to make one long display

Related Curriculum

Language Arts, Social Studies, Art

Materials

- one sheet of white construction paper
- fine-line marker
- cassette or CD player
- recording of soft nature or classical music
- rolls of adding machine tape (precut into 3-foot sections, at least one section for each pair of students)

- pencils, colored pencils, pens, crayons, or markers
- tape

Optional: *I'm in Charge of Celebrations* by Byrd Baylor; stapler or pushpins

Time

Two 40-minute sessions

Preparation

Prior to the activity, make a list of five things you believe are important to celebrate. Make your list as personal as you like. For example, your list might include seeing the first spring flower bloom, biting into a gooey piece of double chocolate cake, or learning that your daughter or son has been accepted by a college.

Write this list on a sheet of construction paper, using a fine-line marker. Keep your list hidden from the students until it is meant to be shared in the lesson.

Activity Steps

1. Set the mood. Turn on the music as students arrive in your classroom or as they prepare to move to this new activity. Don't speak at first; allow 4–5 minutes for students to begin to take in the softness of the sounds they hear.

2. Introduce the activity. Ask students to confer with a neighbor or with other students at their table about the meaning of the word "celebration." Allow 2–3 minutes for students to arrive at a definition of the word with their partners or groups. As students brainstorm, draw two columns on the board, labeled "Definitions" and "Celebrations."

Next, have students (with their partners or groups) name some things that are celebrated. Allow only a few minutes.

3. Discuss celebrations. Select students to share their ideas orally. Write down the ideas in the columns on the board. Again, this should take only a few minutes.

4. Talk about celebrating "small wonders." Explain to students that they will be expanding their concept of what can be celebrated.

If possible, read *I'm in Charge of Celebrations.* During or after the reading, be sure to share the book's intricate illustrations. This book should yield a rich discussion about the need for us to marvel at those times and things in our lives that often seem so small.

Discuss with students the importance of taking time to "stop and smell the roses." Share your list of five things you feel are important to celebrate.

5. Brainstorm in pairs. Divide students into pairs and challenge partners to brainstorm as many things worth celebrating as they can. After eight minutes, have the students pause briefly for each pair to share a favorite celebration from their list. Though students may be eager to share many ideas, you'll want to limit each pair to one response. This allows everyone a chance to participate.

Explain specifically why you like the ideas students shared. Perhaps vocabulary was descriptive, a response was unique, or a thought shed special light on something typically considered mundane.

Encourage students to review their lists and elaborate upon those already written or add more ideas to their lists. Allow 5–7 minutes for this revision.

6. Review lists. Instruct pairs to review their lists and mark with an asterisk (*) the 10 they believe to be the most creative and original.

7. Transfer lists to adding machine tape. Have students transfer their ideas onto adding machine tape and use markers or colored pencils to illustrate and decorate their sections of the tape. Explain that all of the sections will be taped together and displayed for others to read. Allow adequate time for the partners to complete their tapes. Continue to play background music during this work session.

8. Share celebration tapes. Once students are finished, have them sit in a circle and share their designated celebrations. As each pair shares, comment on specific elements, such as descriptive words or creative designs, that you especially like about their celebration tapes. Encourage students to make positive comments about their peers' tapes as well.

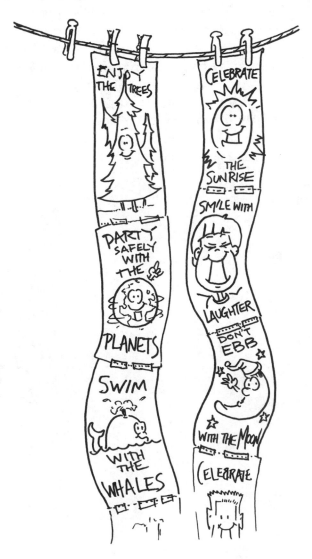

9. Display the tapes. Tape the ends of the sections together to make one long strip. Hang the completed strip as part of a display called "Let's Celebrate!" or "We're in the Mood to Celebrate!"

For Surefire Success

- Getting students into an appropriate frame of mind for this activity is critical, and the softness of nature or classical music really helps. Play it during the group work as students brainstorm, write, and complete their celebration ideas. Also, showing your excitement about everyone's ideas encourages students to seek out creative celebrations that are meaningful to them.

- We have found that an effective way to display the completed tapes is to handle them like crepe-paper streamers: staple or tape them in 12-inch sections and loosely drape them from the ceiling down along the walls. This can be easily accomplished on a suspended ceiling by using a stapler or push-pins. Another idea is to suspend the tapes straight down from the ceiling, like ribbons; they might need an anchor of some type, such as a large paper clip, at the bottom.

Classroom Extensions

- You might wish to use this activity as an introduction to a larger theme or unit of study. Perhaps each month your class can concentrate on one specific thing to celebrate (such as friendship or diversity). Students can write about the topic, create artwork, or do other related activities you assign, which can then be included in your celebrations display.

- If you choose to expand this activity, consider having students select two of their favorite writings or drawings to include in a bound book titled "Our Celebrations." Duplicate the book for students to take home at the end of the year.

School Extension

This activity can easily be expanded to include other classrooms or even the whole school. Think of how wonderful it would be for a visitor to walk into your school and be greeted by a banner announcing "Let's Celebrate!" – and then look up to see yards of decorated adding machine tape clinging to walls and draped from the ceiling!

Thumbnail Sketches

As the school year unfolds, students begin to realize that even though they share many things in common – grade level, age, interests – they also differ in many ways. Indeed, each student is unique. To help students consider this idea and explore it in a creative way, this activity uses each student's one-of-a-kind thumbprint as a central character in a cartoon autobiography. The activity affords class members the opportunity to get to know themselves and each other more fully as they examine why and how every student is "thumbbody" special.

Learning Objectives

Through this activity, students will:

- recognize and appreciate similarities and differences among classmates
- identify personal strengths, interests, and goals
- identify significant people in their lives
- tell personal stories creatively within an assigned framework

Product

Student-created cartoon autobiographies, using thumbprints to create students' images

Related Curriculum

Language Arts, Social Studies, Art

Materials

- eight index cards
- pencils
- ink pads of various colors
- one or two copies of "Storyboard Template" handout (page 68) for each student (see "Preparation")
- overhead projector and transparency made from "Thumbbody's Story" reproducible master (page 69) *or* a few copies to distribute among students
- pens with various colors of ink
- moist towelettes or baby wipes to clean off thumbprints

Optional: laminating material or fixative

For Classroom Extension: The Sneetches and Other Stories by Dr. Seuss *or* the video *Green Eggs and Ham*

For Family Extension: one or more sheets of unlined 8½" x 11" paper for each student

Time

One 30-minute session to introduce the activity; additional at-home or in-class time to create the autobiographies

Preparation

So students will have eight large frames in which to work, photocopy the "Storyboard Template" handout once. Then use the two templates as a master for photocopying 11" x 17" eight-frame sheets (see page 66). Make extra copies so students can perfect their thumbprints and writing.

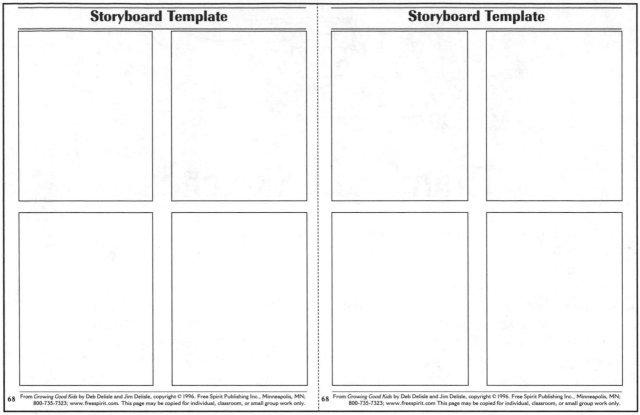

| Storyboard Template | Storyboard Template |

An eight-frame storyboard template.

Activity Steps

1. Pose a riddle. Ask your students: "What is something unique you've had since birth but you probably wouldn't recognize if you saw it?" As students raise their hands to offer responses, invite them to the front of the class to share their answers. Do this until you have 6–8 student volunteers.

Tell your students that among the things that make each of them unique, one that often goes unrecognized throughout people's lives is the individuality of their fingerprints. Even though no one else on earth has the exact same set of lines, creases, and crevices, most people wouldn't know their fingerprints if they came face-to-face (or face-to-print) with them.

2. Make a few thumbprints. Give each volunteer an index card. Ask these students to write their names, in pencil, on the side with lines. Here's where the fun (and a little mess) occurs: Invite each student volunteer to take the right thumb, press it into an ink pad, and transfer the print onto the unlined side of the index card. As the students return to their seats, shuffle the index cards.

3. Try to identify thumbprints. Hold up one card and ask: "Whose print is this?" Inevitably, some students will identify the wrong prints as theirs (and when a fifth-grade boy identifies a girl's print as his own, or vice versa, everyone usually guffaws). This proves your assertion that even though they've had these prints since the day they were born, they still can't recognize them. Then say: "Well, that's about to change!"

4. Introduce the activity. Tell your students that they will each have a chance to become more familiar with their own thumbprint: They will use the print to design a cartoon character. Distribute copies of the "Storyboard Template" handout you have prepared (we call it a "storyboard" because it resembles cartoon frames). Explain that the first frame of the cartoon should read: "Hi! I'm thumbbody special. My name is _____ and I'd like to introduce you to my owner."

From there, it's up to your students' imaginations. The additional storyboard frames can show the thumbprint doing the kinds of things students like to do, visiting the places they've gone or would like to go, envisioning or acting out their plans and dreams. Display or distribute "Thumbbody's Story" so students can see an example of how one of our students developed a thumbnail autobiography.

5. Create thumbprint cartoons. Remind your students that there are no right or wrong ways to do this activity; they may be very creative in both the content and style of their story. For example:

- Students could write their story in poetic form, using rhyme or free verse.

- Students could write their story as a series of riddles ("I like this summer sport that involves water.").

- Students could move through their lives chronologically, writing about what they were like as young children, who they are now, and who they hope to be as adults.

- Students could assume an alias and write as if they had spent their lives as someone else – maybe even a space alien!

Be sure to have extra handouts and plenty of moist towelettes on hand, as there will be some mistakes and smudges. If students want to keep their "Thumbnail Sketches" for posterity, laminate or spray them with fixative as soon as they are complete. Otherwise, the ink will soon smudge.

6. Share and post cartoons. Once the cartoons are completed, give all students a chance to share their stories with other classmates in small groups, round-robin fashion. Later, invite students to display the autobiographies for everyone to read and enjoy.

For Surefire Success

- Try to find ink pads of different colors – black, red, purple, and green are fairly easy to find. Then an "embarrassed" thumbprint can be depicted in red and one that was hit by a hammer can be black and blue. Combining colors into a single smudge yields some interesting results!

- Have students start by doing a rough draft of the storyboard. Then, for their final copy, have them complete the written part of their story first, leaving the thumbprinting for the final step – it's less messy this way. (And if your students are like ours, after starting with the "fun stuff" they'll be less likely to want to write their stories!)

Classroom Extension

As a fun follow-up that can also prompt good discussion about the wonder of individual differences, read the story "The Sneetches" from Dr. Seuss's *The Sneetches and Other Stories* or show the animated version of the story (from the *Green Eggs and Ham* video).

Family Extension

If you're looking for an inexpensive and easy holiday gift for students to create for families and other special people, have them make "Thumbbody Special" stationery. Use 8½" x 11" paper, folded once lengthwise and once widthwise. Their messages might begin with:

- "Grandma and Grandpa, you are both thumbbody special. Here's why:"

- "Paul, as a stepdad, you are thumbbody special. Here's why:"

- "Ming-Le, you are 'thumb' special sister. Here's why:"

Storyboard Template

Thumbbody's Story

Here is a thumbnail cartoon autobiography written by a fifth-grade student:

Filling Our Own Shoes

Goals are inspiring. Thinking of ways to arrive at them, however, is more challenging and, ultimately, more rewarding! Here is an activity that stretches your students' thinking as they explore the specific characteristics required to turn dreams into realities. Use it as a follow-up to "Possible Dreams" (pages 80–81) or as an enrichment activity for a study of leaders and leadership. Students work in teams to create and "fill" shoes with the traits and skills that lead to success. The shoes students craft are larger than life – as are the leaders about whom students are thinking.

Learning Objectives

Through this activity, students will:

- think critically about traits of leadership
- identify qualities of successful people
- consider how to turn dreams into realities
- think and work cooperatively

Product

Large shoes (approximately 3' x 5') constructed by student teams

Related Curriculum

Language Arts, Social Studies, Art

Materials

- overhead projector and transparency made from "One Filled Shoe" reproducible master (page 72) *or* copies for each team of three students
- large sheets (approximately 3' x 5') of white butcher paper (one sheet for each team of three students)
- scissors

- markers, pens, or fine-line markers
- other decorative art materials such as paints, shoelaces, ribbons, glitter

Time

Two or three 40-minute sessions

Preparation

Before class begins, write the following questions on the board:

- What does it mean to "follow in someone else's footsteps"?
- What does it mean when someone says, "Those are hard shoes to fill"?

Activity Steps

1. Introduce the activity. After students are settled, ask them to ponder the questions on the board. Depending upon your room arrangement, you might invite them to discuss the possible meanings of these statements in quotations with one or two other students, or with the other students at their table. Allow 5–10 minutes for the discussion.

2. Discuss the ideas as a class. Solicit ideas and write them on the board. Lead a carefully orchestrated discussion in which you help students to unravel the meaning of these two statements. You might wish to provide specific examples in which each might be made.

Move the discussion to a higher level by asking:

- What kinds of characteristics are generally associated with people we admire? With people we consider to be leaders? With people who are successful?

- How do you think these people achieved their status or goals?

It isn't necessary to get into an in-depth discussion about the definitions of "leadership" or "success." Your purpose is to have students generate a list of characteristics. Again, list these ideas on the board. You might wish to categorize the ideas into specific topics, such as characteristics, personality, or work ethics.

Now have students revisit the two questions originally discussed. Explore extensions of their original ideas.

3. Personalize the ideas in small groups. Divide students into teams of three. Challenge them to think of ways that they can "fill their own shoes." Display or distribute the example provided in "One Filled Shoe." If your class needs more specifics, you might wish to designate a certain number of personality characteristics (such as honesty) and a specific number of strategies (such as taking risks) to include on their shoes.

This step of the activity requires a good deal of guidance because many students will be content with their initial thinking. Encourage students to really consider the traits that lead to success and the challenges leaders may have encountered in their lives. Monitor groups and encourage the members to stretch their thinking.

When the teams have finished this step, ask them to mark with an asterisk (*) the ideas that represent their best thinking. These are the ideas that they will include on their shoe. You should review this list.

4. Design and create shoes. Have groups plan the design for their shoes. Stress that they are to be as creative as possible, and that the design of the shoe should reflect the personalities of all of the group's members. After approving the design, distribute the paper and other art supplies and give the go-ahead for the students to construct their shoes.

5. Share the finished products with the class. Provide an opportunity for the teams to share their work and ideas with others.

6. Display the shoes. These shoes will make a wonderful display, whether suspended from the ceiling of your classroom or "marching" along the walls of the school hallways.

For Surefire Success

You might introduce this lesson by having a student interview you as you role-play a leader you admire or think your students would find interesting. If you choose to do this, prepare ahead of time a series of questions for the student interviewer to use. These questions should focus on your journey toward "greatness."

Classroom Extension

You can easily adapt this activity to fit into a lesson on specific people (perhaps as a conclusion for a unit on biographies) or within a specific area (such as "scientists"). If you choose to use this lesson as a connection to a specific topic or unit of study, you might direct each group to focus on one specific individual. For example, during a study of U.S. presidents, each group could select a little-known president and include personality characteristics, barriers he overcame, and goals he achieved.

One Filled Shoe

Here is a shoe inspired by a team of fourth-grade students:

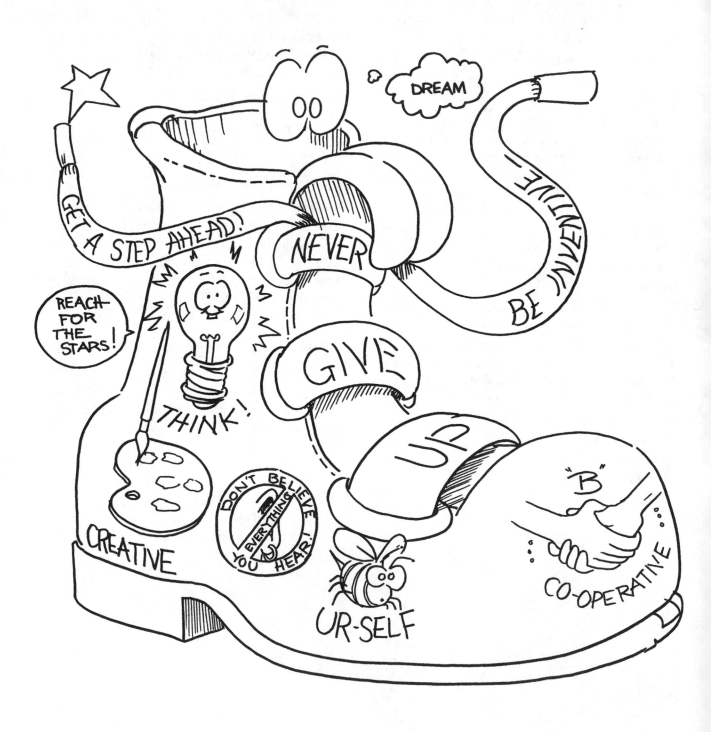

The Ultimate Vacation

Who doesn't fantasize about taking a dream vacation? Yet, in the real world, who doesn't travel on a budget? Give your students an opportunity to put themselves in both positions as they imagine "the ultimate vacation" and work together to plan and role-play a down-to-earth outing on a predetermined budget. Beyond the enjoyment this activity affords, it invites students to explore personal interests, values, and dreams and to gain insight into their own and their classmates' hearts and minds.

Use the activity before an extended school break to give a creative, witty, and resourceful outlet to students' pent-up energy.

Learning Objectives

Through this activity, students will:
- think creatively and spontaneously
- discuss and solve problems
- experience a cooperative way to reach a consensus
- explore their own and their classmates' values

Product

Student-produced skits depicting creative ways to spend vacations on a variety of budgets

Related Curriculum

Language Arts, Social Studies, Math

Materials

- two sheets of cardboard or fluorescent posterboard, each at least 18" x 22"
- scissors
- markers
- two brass fasteners
- overhead projector and transparency made from "What Does It Cost?" reproducible master (page 76) *or* copies for each group of 4–5 students

Time

One 50-minute session; additional in-school time to perform skits

Preparation

Follow the directions to make a "Wheel of Fantasy" (representing a variety of ideas for possible vacation locales) and a "Wheel of Fortune" (representing widely varying amounts of money). Examples of finished wheels are shown on page 74.

1. Cut cardboard or fluorescent posterboard into two 18-inch circles. Divide each circle into eight segments.

2. For the "Wheel of Fantasy," write a different vacation locale in each segment. Use both real and imaginary destinations, such as Walt Disney World, Grandma's house, Mars, Never-Never Land, or your school.

3. For the "Wheel of Fortune," write a different sum of money in each segment, from $0 to $1 million.

4. Cut two cardboard spinners in the shape of arrows; attach the spinners to the wheels using brass fasteners.

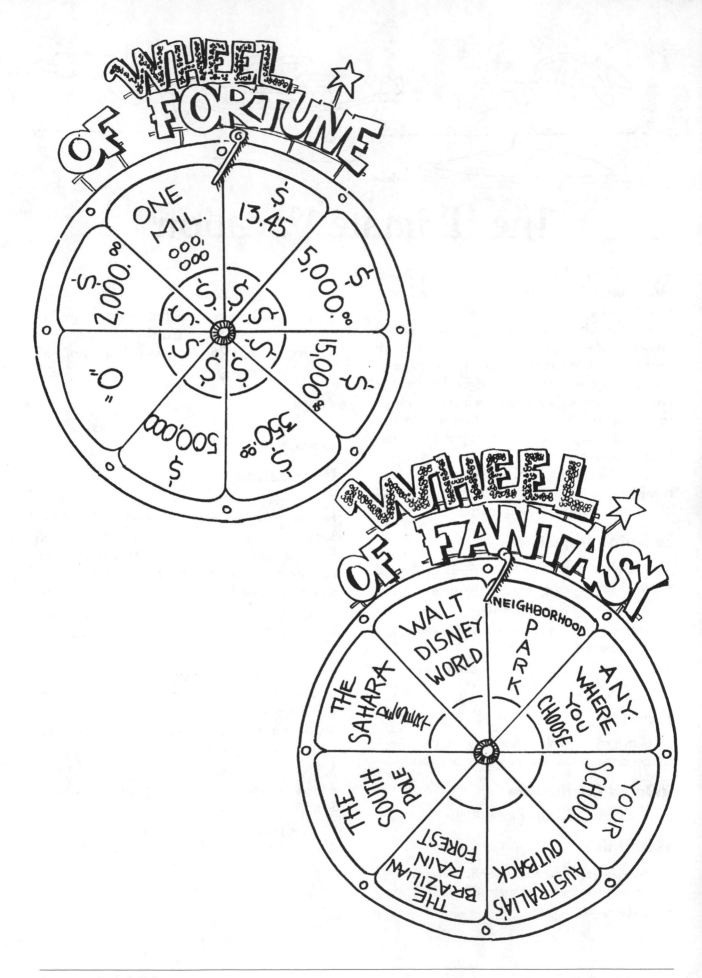

Activity Steps

1. Introduce the activity. Ask your students about their plans for the upcoming break or for a future vacation. On the board, write each of the places and activities the students name, from the mundane (hanging out at home) to the exotic (relaxing on a tropical island).

2. Talk about "the ultimate vacation." Invite students' ideas about where they would go on "the ultimate vacation," for which money would be no object and the destination could be anywhere at all. Ask: "Where would you go? What would you do? Who would go with you? Parents? Siblings? Friends? Favorite celebrities?" Encourage students to elaborate on the many things they would see and do.

Next, tell students that even though you can't promise them everything they might hope for in their dream vacations, you *can* promise them a little bit of adventure through this activity.

3. Spin the wheels. Display the "Wheel of Fortune" and the "Wheel of Fantasy." Assuming your best carnival barker tone of voice ("'Round and 'round and 'round it goes – where it stops, nobody knows!"), invite a student to spin one of the wheels; invite a second student to spin the other. Ask these two students what kinds of things they could do at this destination given the budget they have. Invite ideas from the rest of the class as well. Once you've exhausted the possibilities, ask for volunteers to perform a spontaneous skit that highlights what this vacation might be like.

4. Form small groups. Split your students into "traveling groups" of 4–5 people. Have each team spin the wheels once. Explain that they are to plan a trip to the destination spun on the "Wheel of Fantasy," a trip filled with activities that fit the budget that Lady Luck gave them on the "Wheel of Fortune." Display or distribute the "What Does It Cost?" handout and briefly review typical vacation costs with students.

5. Plan vacation skits. Allow groups approximately 20 minutes to plan and practice a skit about how they will spend their luck-of-the-draw vacation. Remind students that they must be very creative in figuring out how to get to their destination, where they will stay once they arrive, what they will see and do, where and what they will eat. Explain that every group member must participate in some way in the presentation. Remind groups: "You must stick to your budget!"

6. Perform skits. Once the time is up, invite students to perform their skits for the class. Then sit back, relax, and think of all the things that you will be doing on your own upcoming break – even if it won't be the vacation of your dreams!

For Surefire Success

- Limit group size to 4–5 students and make sure that every student has a role, however small, to play. With more than five students per group, you are likely to see a lot of silliness and other off-task behavior.

- Circulate among the groups to answer questions about costs not included on the "What Does It Cost?" sheet. Groups, particularly those with very little to spend, may not know how much is too much.

Classroom Extension

If your students enjoy this activity, do a more serious takeoff on it. Select some of society's most pressing problems (such as drug abuse, homelessness, air or water pollution, violence) and create a "Wheel of Friction" to use with the "Wheel of Fortune." Have students write out plans for helping to solve this problem within their given budget. Students may want to enact these solutions in a skit, but a written account of their ideas will encourage more substantial thought. Students might be surprised at how much they can accomplish to solve a problem, even with a small budget.

What Doe$ It ¢o$t?

Use this chart for reference when figuring out your vacation expenses:

TRANSPORTATION	$	¢	$	$	¢	¢	$	¢	¢	
Round-trip air fare to any place in your own country/continent										$ 400
Round-trip air fare to any place overseas										$ 1,200
Round-trip train fare to any place in your own country/continent										$ 250
Round-trip bus fare to any place in your own country/continent										$ 200
New bicycle										$ 150
Stay at home and explore your own town/city										FREE

LODGING	$	¢	$	$	¢	¢	$	¢	¢	
1 night at a fancy hotel or resort in a big city										$ 250
1 night at a fancy hotel or resort in a small town										$ 200
1 night at a mid-price hotel or motel in a big city										$ 150
1 night at a mid-price hotel or motel in a small town										$ 100
1 night at a YMCA or hostel										$ 25
Sleep at home or at a relative's or friend's home										FREE

MEALS	$	¢	$	$	¢	¢	$	¢	¢	
1 day's meals at fancy restaurants										$ 150
1 day's meals at mid-price restaurants										$ 40
1 day's fast-food meals										$ 15
1 day of brown bagging										$ 10
Eat at home or at a relative's or friend's home										FREE

OTHER EXPENSES	$	¢	$	$	¢	¢	$	¢	¢	
1 day's pass to a major amusement park										$ 60
1 ticket to a classical music concert										$ 35
1 ticket to a rock concert										$ 30
1 ticket to a zoo										$ 10
1 ticket to a museum										$ 5
1 ticket to a museum on free admission day										FREE

Fill in other activities and estimated costs:

_____ $ ____

_____ $ ____

_____ $ ____

Good Things Come to Those Who Wait

A great challenge of teaching is to help our students recognize that time, effort, and patience are essential to personal success. In a culture of instant gratification, it's difficult for students to view time as something deliberate, focused, and purposeful. As students examine their own personal activities and goals, they begin to better understand that life's richest experiences depend upon the wise use of time – to reflect, to ponder, to work, and, sometimes, to wait.

Learning Objectives

Through this activity, students will:
- identify activities worthy of consideration
- work and think cooperatively
- identify personal values, interests, and goals
- evaluate ideas and offer constructive, positive feedback
- understand that reaching long-term goals takes both effort and time
- recognize that waiting can yield positive results

Product

Student-created lists of ideas about important things in life that take time

Related Curriculum

Language Arts, Social Studies, Art

Materials

- chart paper or newsprint (two sheets for each group of 3–4 students)
- overhead projector and transparency made from "Patience Pays" reproducible master (page 79) *or* copy for each group of students
- pencils, colored pencils, pens, crayons, markers, or paints
- other decorative art materials for illustrating the lists

For Variation: materials for making books (see "Four Ways to Make a Book," pages 33–36)

Time

One or two 40-minute sessions, depending upon the depth of the class discussions

Activity Steps

1. Introduce the activity. Begin by writing on the board: "Good things come to those who wait." Ask students to explain what they think the statement means. Expand their thinking by encouraging them to consider what it could mean from a variety of perspectives. For example, what might the statement mean to an NBA basketball star? To a scientist? To a parent? List students' ideas on the board. Limit this discussion to 5 minutes.

After students share their ideas, discuss the concept of waiting. It is important for students to recognize that waiting is not necessarily a passive activity. Rather, it can be a meaningful period in which ideas form, talents develop, or spring bulbs blossom!

2. Brainstorm ideas in small groups. Divide the class into groups of 3–4 students. Give each group a sheet of chart paper or newsprint. Explain that they will have 10 minutes to brainstorm a list of things that take time.

After 10 minutes, stop the groups and display or distribute "Patience Pays"; share and discuss just a few items from this list. Encourage students to use these examples as a springboard for adding to and enhancing their own ideas. It is effective to share some of the more abstract ideas (becoming wise, learning to be a good friend) so that your students will be encouraged to think beyond the obvious.

Challenge groups to return to their lists for 10 more minutes to add ideas. If students feel "stuck," remind them that as their thinking hits a plateau, they should keep going: New ideas will eventually surface. After 10 minutes, have groups share their completed lists with the class. Ask for positive feedback. What item on each list is the most creative? The most meaningful? What item represents something others would like to gain by waiting (for example, a new friend, a goal)?

3. Talk about reaching goals. Have a class discussion about goals and the process used to reach them. Interject the notions of both short-term and long-term goals. Also, help students identify those meaningful aspects in our lives (peace, friendship) that can't be purchased but do require time and patience to cultivate. You may also like to have students explore the difficulty of waiting, which requires patience and trust.

4. Create final lists. Give each group clean sheets of chart paper or newsprint. Tell groups to select from their brainstormed ideas 15 items they consider most important. Explain that they are to list these on clean sheets and add illustrations to make their chart visually appealing.

5. Display the lists. Arrange the lists on a wall or bulletin board under the title "Good Things Come to Those Who Wait."

For Surefire Success

- Sit in on each brainstorming group and offer a specific idea, especially one that involves an abstract concept, to encourage students to expand their thinking.
- Challenge students to think beyond the obvious. Coax them away from materialistic goals. Depending upon your students, you might consider limiting the number of items or activities that involve money.

Classroom Extension

Leave room for additions to the lists. Encourage students to add, as they think of them, more good ideas of things in life that take time.

Variations

- Create a single long chart for display in the hallway.
- Compile the lists into a book format (see "Four Ways to Make a Book." Duplicate the book and provide everyone with a copy.

Patience Pays

A group of sixth graders developed this list:

These things take time...

 **baking a cake**

writing a symphony

■ learning to be a good friend

■ watching a sunset

■ listening to a child's story

■ building a home

■ learning a different language

turning coal into diamonds

■ becoming wise

■ growing into an adult

making the planet a healthier place

 **pretending**

■ earning money

■ knowing oneself

■ reading a mystery book

From *Growing Good Kids* by Deb Delisle and Jim Delisle, copyright © 1996. Free Spirit Publishing Inc., Minneapolis, MN; 800-735-7323; www.freespirit.com. This page may be copied for individual, classroom, or small group work only.

Possible Dreams

Your students' adventures in daydreaming have already begun. This activity allows them to harness their goals and help realize them, starting today. Through the example of a talented individual who pursued his daydreams, students see the possibilities within themselves to pursue theirs. From there, they begin their own adventures in charting life goals. As your students proceed through this activity, you will gain keen insights into their minds and the hopes and goals they harbor.

Learning Objectives

Through this activity, students will:

- recognize the importance of setting goals
- contemplate and set goals for themselves
- think critically and creatively about life events to which they aspire

Product

Student-created "dream" lists of places they wish to visit, adventures they wish to explore, people they wish to meet, and things they wish to learn within their lifetimes

Related Curriculum

Language Arts, Social Studies

Materials

- overhead projector and transparencies made from "John Goddard's Daydreams and Goals" and "One Student's Possible Dreams" reproducible masters (pages 84–86) or copies for each student
- copies of "My Personal Goals and Possible Dreams" handout (page 87) for each student
- colored pencils, crayons, or markers

Optional: *Kayaks Down the Nile* by John Goddard; faded and patched blue jeans, flannel shirt, and hiking boots; for men, a three-day growth of beard; *Happy Birthday to U.S.: Activities for the Bicentennial* by Murray Suid and Roberta Suid

Time

One 45-minute session to introduce the activity; additional at-home or in-school time to write goals

Background

John Goddard is a man of many accomplishments. In his lifetime, he has scaled Mts. Rainier and Fuji as well as the Matterhorn. He has retraced Marco Polo's route through the Orient and has swum in Africa's Lake Victoria. He has landed and taken off from an aircraft carrier and has piloted high-speed planes, including an F-111. He has earned the rank of Eagle Scout and has learned to play both the flute and the violin. Obviously, Goddard is big on adventure – and on goals.

One of Goddard's greatest accomplishments, and the one about which he wrote his book, *Kayaks Down the Nile*, was the time he and two friends kayaked the entire length of the Nile River (4,145 miles). This nine-month voyage was filled with adventures with the flora, fauna, animals, and people of Africa.

Activity Steps

1. Introduce the activity. The best thing about this activity is that it gives you an excuse to dress up as someone else and impress your students with your versatility. In costume, introduce yourself by name, and ask if your students know who you are. (Trust us, they won't!)

2. Tell about Goddard's experience traveling the Nile. Then, in character, begin to detail some of your accomplishments, using the excerpts from *Kayaks Down the Nile* (see "Nile River Adventures," pages 82–83).

3. Share Goddard's other goals. Once you have finished detailing your kayaking trip, tell the students that this adventure was neither your first nor your last. In fact, the reason you took this challenging trip in the first place was that when you were 15 years old you made up a list of 127 daydreams and goals you wanted to accomplish in your lifetime. Add that over the years your list has grown to include 227 dreams and goals.

Display or distribute "John Goddard's Daydreams and Goals," which highlights some of the goals Goddard has accomplished over a span of more than 55 years. Invite comments and questions on any goals that seem particularly interesting. Tell students that Goddard, who is still alive, has realized more than three-quarters of the goals and dreams he set for himself. (Among the dreams he still hopes to fulfill is number 125, visiting the moon. For a complete list of Goddard's original 127 daydreams and goals, see *Happy Birthday to U.S.*)

Display or distribute "One Student's Possible Dreams," which shows one of our seventh-grade student's goals and daydreams. Briefly discuss the list with students; suggest that they use it to spark their own ideas about feats both large and small that they wish to accomplish in their lives.

4. Write personal goals. Give each student a copy of the "My Personal Goals and Possible Dreams" handout. Challenge students to devise their own individual lists of lifetime possibilities. What places do they hope to visit? Whom would they like to meet? What would they like to learn to do? What would they like to explore, study, read, eat, experience? The list can be endless, and the categories are limited only by students' imaginations. Tell students to organize, format, and decorate their lists in whatever way they wish.

Ask students to try to think beyond meeting people who have only recently become famous. Otherwise, you'll end up getting the athlete or performer *du jour* on each student's wish list. Perhaps they can think of people in categories other than sports or media; give some possible examples from history or current events to help them get started.

Tell students they will have one week to compile their lists. During this time, they are to spend at least 15 minutes each day thinking about and writing down ideas. (Whether this is done during class time or at home is up to you.)

5. Share personal goals. When a week has passed, have the students bring in their lists and share them in groups of 3–4 people. Finally, have each student ask a witness to sign the list. Tell students to take these lists home and keep them someplace safe.

For Surefire Success

- By taking on the character of John Goddard yourself, you will greatly enhance this activity. Kids love it when their teacher dresses up as someone else – it lets them see both your playfulness and your ingenuity. Make sure to stay in character and take your role seriously. Your students really will see you as the person you're pretending to be.

- Make up your own list and share it (in total or part) with your students. This shows them that even though adults have "grown up," they continue to have goals, too.

Classroom Extension

Suggest that students use the goals as the start of personal journals.

Variation

At the beginning of the year, term, or vacation break, have students write letters to themselves detailing their goals for the term ahead. Collect the letters and, at the middle of the term, mail them to students.

Nile River Adventures

Here are five excerpts adapted from John Goddard's *Kayaks Down the Nile*:

Swept Away

As I headed straight into the jungle ahead, I lay back as far as I could to avoid the tangle of vines and limbs clogging the channel. I had just flattened myself when the kayak crashed to a halt deep in the growth. Submerged roots snagged my boat, causing it to heel over sharply. Instantly the torrent rushed over the tilted craft, filling and engulfing it. As the kayak settled, it overturned and broke free of the vines.

I found myself being dragged along upside down in the seething water. I tried to break free, but my legs were ensnared in the lashings that held the bags. Though I had been a skin diver from the age of 12, with good lung capacity, I was in poor condition for the heart-bursting ordeal that followed. For several days I had been suffering from an attack of dysentery that had sapped my vitality, and what strength remained had been squandered in an exhausting escape from some hippos.

I forced myself to make one last try to break free, and with all my strength finally managed to do so. As I kicked away from the kayak, I was seized by the madly swirling water, which buffeted and bowled me along with such overwhelming force that I was completely powerless and too disoriented to determine the direction of the surface. I was swept along like a straw, rolling from one turbulence to another, scraping over reefs, colliding with rocks, desperately fighting to get my head above water.

The raging current tore at my hat, and the strap, still tightly fastened around my chin, was strangling me. With both hands I tore it off. My heavy boots were dragging me down like lead weights. I clawed at them frantically to tear them from my feet, but I couldn't do it. I was drowning. "So this is the way I go," I thought, "like a fly sucked down a drain."

Then, just as my lungs were ready to explode, my head broke the surface. For a glorious moment I breathed in delicious gulps of air, then was sucked under again; but the brief respite was all I needed. I was angry and determined to survive, and I fought back to the surface again, using only my arms – kicking my feet just seemed to make matters worse – and I managed to keep from going under again.

The Hippo

Late this afternoon, as I tramped through the tall grass near our tent, I suddenly came face-to-face with a grazing hippo. He gave a surprised grunt, wheeled around, and headed for the river at a fast jog. Every year hippos kill quite a few people in Africa, a good percentage of them on land, so it seemed a wise idea to keep my specimen on the run before he got any pugnacious ideas and reversed his course. I let out a blood-curdling whoop and charged after him at top speed. I already knew that hippos were marvelously fast swimmers, but it seemed incredible that on land, with no water to support their ponderous bulk, they could also be swift runners. Yet pounding after this one all the way back to the river, I couldn't keep up with him – much less close the gap between us.

I didn't give up the chase until the hippo, stumpy legs driving like pistons, plunged head-long into the river and disappeared under the waves. It was a foolhardy stunt, I know, but with a certain poetic justice to it. And how refreshing it was to be the pursuer for a change, rather than the pursued!

Driver Ants

The highly carnivorous driver ants are the most feared insects of Africa. Every living creature, from fleas to humans, is potential prey to them. They can goad an elephant into a panicky dash for the nearest water when they swarm into its trunk; and they can envelop and consume a large python that has been rendered helpless from eating an antelope or a pig.

In search of food, the ants travel in groups of at least 100,000, moving in long columns three or four inches wide. These hunting parties attack and eat everything they can overwhelm, first assaulting the eyes so that their victims are blinded and unable to find an escape.

One of the most painful episodes of the ongoing battle between us and the insects – which they persisted in winning – was an attack while we were eating our lunch. A column of driver ants descended on us without warning, racing up our bare legs and biting us with their sharp, hooklike mouths. We hopped around in a frenzy, trying to brush them off, but there was no defense against their numbers. We grabbed our loads and fled the area.

The Shampoo

Shilluk men have their hair dressed before important events in their lives. The work is done by the village barber, a highly respected personage whose profession is hereditary and second in importance only to cattle raising.

The actual operation begins with the barber shaving half the customer's head, then shampooing the remaining hair with cow's urine. While the hair steams in the hot sun for a few minutes, the barber prepares a special pomade in a large clay bowl, pounding and stirring an exotic blend of black mud, gum arabica, and cow manure into a thick paste.

This malodorous mixture is smeared onto the customer's head and kneaded into the warm, moist hair; then the desired hairdo is skillfully molded into shape before the hair dries out and hardens. The final touch is a dusting of cow manure and red dye.

It Has Been Done!

I felt a deep sadness at leaving the Nile. It had so totally dominated our lives and had been the supreme subject of our thoughts, plans, dreams, and energies for so many months that it didn't seem possible we were leaving it for good. For so long we had awakened each morning to behold its gleaming expanse leading endlessly to the next horizon. It had borne us thousands of miles through many of the earth's wildest regions. Its waters had cleansed, cooled, and provided sustenance for our bodies. We had been enthralled by its beauty, enraged by its perversity, awed by its magnitude, and frightened by its power. In short, we had just finished the greatest experience of our lives, and I was sorry to see it come to an end.

I had had a personal motto about exploring the Nile: "It should be done. It can be done. It shall be done." Now, at last, I could add, "It has been done!"

John Goddard's Daydreams and Goals

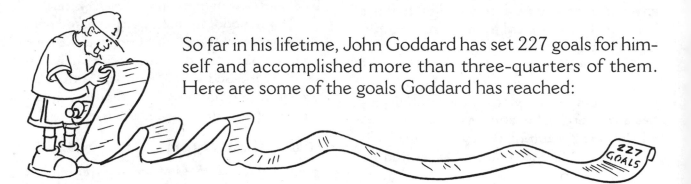

So far in his lifetime, John Goddard has set 227 goals for himself and accomplished more than three-quarters of them. Here are some of the goals Goddard has reached:

- Explore the Nile, Amazon, Congo, and Rio Coco Rivers.

- Climb Mts. Kilimanjaro, Ararat, Rainier, Fuji, and Vesuvius.

- Swim in Lakes Victoria, Superior, Tanganyika, Titicaca, and Nicaragua.

- Explore the Great Barrier Reef, Red Sea, Fiji Islands, Okefenokee Swamp, and Everglades.

- Carry out careers in medicine and exploration.

- Learn fencing and jujitsu.

- Build a telescope.

- Write a book and an article for *National Geographic Magazine*.

- Run a mile in five minutes.

- Learn French, Spanish, and Arabic.

- Pilot a plane, motorcycle, tractor, and canoe.

- Become skilled in using a surfboard, football, basketball, lariat, and boomerang.

- Read the works of Dickens, Emerson, Hemingway, Longfellow, Plato, Poe, Rousseau, Shakespeare, Tolstoy, and Twain.

- Become familiar with the music of Bach, Beethoven, Debussy, Ravel, Rachmaninoff, Rimsky-Korsakov, Tchaikovsky, and Verdi.

- Circumnavigate the globe (he has – four times).

- Marry and have children (he has five).

One Student's Possible Dreams

Here is a goal list created by a seventh-grade student:

Places to explore

1. The North Pole
2. Every U.S. state
3. An Indian reservation in Arizona
4. The Great Barrier Reef
5. The attic of a haunted house
6. A castle in England
7. The Oval Office

Things to learn to do

1. Scuba dive
2. Create a cartoon character
3. Surf
4. Invent a video game
5. Drive a car with a stick shift

People to meet

1. A past U.S. president
2. My uncle who lives in Israel
3. The Chicago Bulls
4. Oprah Winfrey
5. The owner of a movie studio

Physical accomplishments

1. Run a mile in less than four minutes
2. Build a treehouse by myself
3. Walk through every country in Asia
4. Eat nothing but candy for one week
5. Outrun a dangerous animal that's chasing me

Other goals

1. Appear in a horror movie

2. Have three kids and two dogs

3. Invent something that will stop pollution

4. Open a video store

5. Whitewater raft

6. Spit off the top of the Eiffel Tower

7. Meet Steven Spielberg

8. Own a red sports car

9. Connect the moon and the earth with paper clips

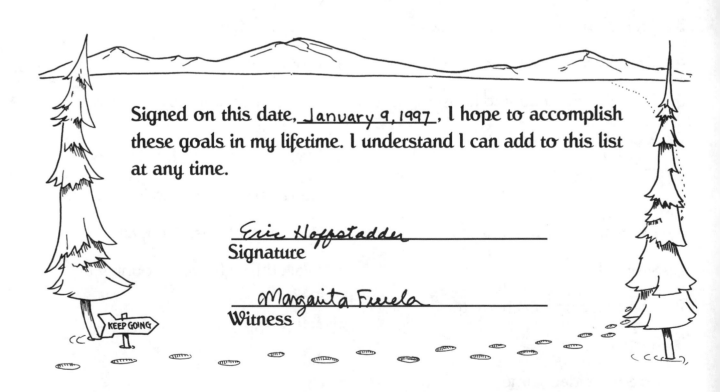

Signed on this date, _January 9, 1997_, I hope to accomplish these goals in my lifetime. I understand I can add to this list at any time.

Eric Hoffstadden
Signature

Margarita Fuuela
Witness

KEEP GOING

My Personal Goals and Possible Dreams

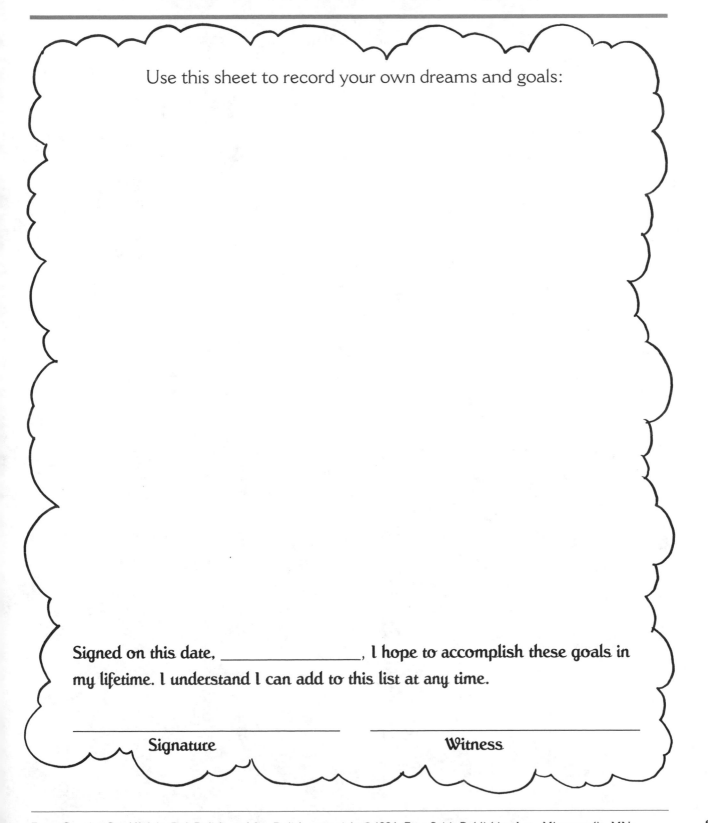

Use this sheet to record your own dreams and goals:

Signed on this date, _____, I hope to accomplish these goals in my lifetime. I understand I can add to this list at any time.

_____   _____
Signature   Witness

Activities for Growing with the World

365 Days of Helping Others

Many people, both adults and children, make New Year's resolutions. What better focus for students' resolutions than on ways to make positive changes at home, with friends, at school, and in their community? What better medium for recording resolutions than a calendar? A calendar is useful again and again. Every 30 days or so, it gives the person using it something different and fresh to look at and to ponder.

Here's an activity that calls on students to consider ways to help other people 365 days a year. We introduce this project right after Thanksgiving, when students are already in a holiday mood, counting the days until their extended winter break. An added benefit of this group project is that the calendar makes a perfect holiday gift.

Learning Objectives

Through this activity, students will:

- define realistic goals
- work cooperatively toward a broad goal
- work creatively within a standard format
- consider and set personal commitments
- plan and carry out a project over several days

Product

Student-designed calendar focused around themes of global awareness and respect

Related Curriculum

Social Studies, Art, Language Arts

Materials

- overhead projector and transparency made from "Themes for Helping Month by Month" reproducible master (page 93)
- several sheets of unlined 8½" x 11" paper for each group of 2–8 students
- several copies of "Calendar Template" handout (page 94) for each group of students
- a sampling of calendars for the coming year and from current or past years
- crayons or markers
- pencils
- fine-line markers
- binding machine *or* paper punch, and yarn *or* stapler

Time

One 30-minute session to introduce the activity; additional at-home and in-school time to complete it

Activity Steps

1. Introduce the activity. To begin, write these sentences on the board: "I'll lose 15 pounds." "I'll exercise more." "I'll make one new friend." "I'll try to be more patient." Ask students if they've ever heard anyone say any of these statements. Then ask:

- What do these statements have in common?
- At what time of year do you usually hear statements like these?

Inevitably, several students will mention New Year's resolutions. Ask if anyone's family makes resolutions collectively or if family members do so independently. Students can provide examples. Next, ask if anyone has ever made any New Year's resolutions such as "I'll improve my grades," "I won't fight with my sister," or "I'll do my homework."

Then ask: "How long do these resolutions usually last? How long does it take before the dieter nibbles at a piece of chocolate cake, or a big brother yells at his sister for messing with his Nintendo?" Your students will get the hint: Usually, resolutions last only as long as one's willpower can tolerate the change.

Finish the introduction by telling your students: "Today we're going to plan for the future – your future – by making some resolutions that might really last all year. We'll base our resolutions on promises that are worth keeping, and we'll put them into a calendar so you'll have daily reminders of your good intentions."

2. Form groups. Divide students into 12 working groups. (These groups can include 2–8 members, depending on whether you do the activity with a class of 25 or a team of 100.) Show students the "Themes for Helping Month by Month" transparency (or, if you wish, decide with students on 12 topics of interest to them). Explain that each group will be responsible for creating a calendar page for one month. Assign or let each group select a month and a topic.

Give each group sheets of paper and copies of the "Calendar Template" handout. Make the sample calendars you have collected available to all groups so students can get ideas for illustrations or designs.

3. Create the calendar. This is a lot of work, and it will take several small-group meetings to accomplish. One suggested way to divide the work is as follows:

Task A: Illustrate

Design an illustration that will fit on an 8½" x 11" sheet and that corresponds to the month's theme.

Task B: Note days, dates, and holidays

On the "Calendar Template" handout, label the month and days and number the dates. Place all national, state, religious, and school holidays in the appropriate spaces on the calendar. For best results, tell students to print lightly with a pencil first, check the spelling, and then print over the pencil with a black, fine-line marker.

Task C: Create resolutions

For the remaining calendar days (those that are not holidays), devise resolutions that fit the month's theme, such as "Invite a new kid to sleep over" or "Recycle your *Weekly Readers*." Suggest that for some days of each month, groups include illustrations instead of words. For example, a picture of two kids shaking hands (representing making friends or making mutual decisions) could occupy a day or two for a given month.

Groups working on different months may come up with similar ideas for some days. Assure students that this is okay. After all, some good resolutions are worth repeating!

4. Create a cover for the calendar. Appoint or have students appoint a committee of 3–4 students to design a cover for the calendar that represents many of the ideas reflected on its pages. Perhaps some of your class's artists will volunteer for this task.

5. Assemble the calendar. Your finished product will be a monthly calendar, 11" x 17", with a spiral bind in the middle. If you do not have access to a binding machine, connect the pages with yarn or staple them.

Be sure to keep a set of unbound originals for duplicating more copies of the calendar. If you have access to a color copier, all the better!

6. Distribute calendars. Distribute copies of the calendar for students' personal use or for presenting as holiday gifts to friends and family.

For Surefire Success

- Have students brainstorm multiple ideas for their calendar pages before completing their final copy. Distribute several copies of the "Calendar Template" handout so groups can plan their month's dates accurately.

- Encourage students to balance serious and humorous resolutions. Do not allow inappropriate topics.

- Before completing a final copy, have an editor (perhaps you or a parent volunteer) review spelling, grammar, and appropriateness of content.

School Extensions

- Use the calendars as a fund-raising item for a school or community project.

- Provide the principal, superintendent, and school board members with copies. This is great PR!

Themes for Helping Month by Month

JANUARY
Keeping healthy so we can
help others

FEBRUARY
Increasing our understanding
of people who differ from us

MARCH
Improving our relationships
with friends or siblings

APRIL
Cleaning up or improving
the environment

MAY
Bringing small rays of sunshine
into people's lives

JUNE
Improving relationships
with parents

JULY
Celebrating our own backgrounds
and our nation's heritage

AUGUST
Keeping cool
when tempers get hot

SEPTEMBER
Setting and maintaining
good attitudes toward school

OCTOBER
Making the world
a less scary place

NOVEMBER
Showing thanks to people
we care about

DECEMBER
Being generous
to others

Calendar Template

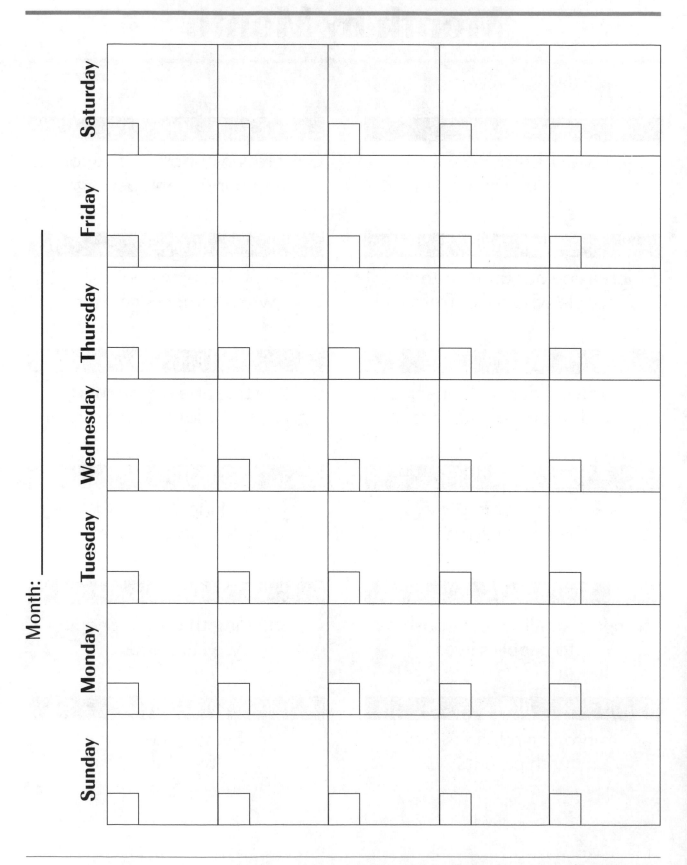

Month: _____

| Sunday | Monday | Tuesday | Wednesday | Thursday | Friday | Saturday |

Heart to Heart

Many students are naturally inclined to reach out to others. This activity enables students to reach out to individuals whom they have never met via written communication. By offering messages of hope and optimism to strangers, students come to recognize empathy as an important feeling to develop and nurture. Additionally, the art of writing letters takes on a new and relevant meaning for your students.

Learning Objectives

Through this activity, students will:

- recognize the needs of others
- empathize with people whom they do not know personally
- recognize and act on their own capacity to support other people
- work and think cooperatively
- compose and write letters of support and encouragement

Product

Cut-out hearts that contain newspaper clippings and student responses

Related Curriculum

Language Arts, Social Studies, Art

Materials

- one or two newspaper sections (no older than one week) for each pair of students
- overhead projector and transparency made from "Heartfelt Communication" reproducible master (page 98) *or* copies for each pair of students

- writing paper
- large sheet of red construction paper for each pair of students
- scissors
- paste or glue
- envelopes and stamps

Optional: *Miss Rumphius* by Barbara Cooney

For Classroom and School Extension: map, pushpins, small hearts to pin to the map

Time

One or two 40-minute sessions

Preparation

Select and clip a newspaper story or picture that describes people doing something positive for others. Also select and clip one additional newspaper piece that will easily elicit a feeling of concern or empathy and a desire to offer support and hope.

Activity Steps

1. Introduce the activity. Start by sharing the first newspaper article or picture you selected – your "good news" clipping. Invite students to comment on what the person or activity has done to make the world a better place.

Optional: If you have a copy of *Miss Rumphius,* read this story to your students and discuss the three lessons Miss Rumphius's grandfather taught her. Ask students to comment on the last lesson, described as the most important one by her grandfather: to make the world a more beautiful place.

2. Discuss ideas for making a better world. Ask students: "What are some ways adults and children can make the world a more beautiful place?" List students' ideas on the board in two categories, "Adults" and "Children/Young People."

After students have generated sizable lists, review their ideas. Have them identify some differences and similarities between the two categories' entries. Discuss those that require a significant amount of money in order to be accomplished; place dollar signs ($$) next to those activities. Decide which require little or no money; place an asterisk (*) next to those. (If there are none requiring little money, suggest adding a couple to the list, such as "Make 10 new friends over the course of five years" or "Shovel snow for a neighbor without being paid for it.")

Explain to students that you will all be taking on the challenge of making the world a more beautiful place.

3. Group students in pairs. Divide the class into pairs. Distribute one or two newspaper sections to pairs. Explain that each pair is to locate a picture or an article that interests them, one that could warrant a positive response such as a compliment or note of support.

Provide two specific examples to students, using both the clipping you have already shown and the other one you selected in your preparation. Make sure students understand that they may select either type of news, as long as they can think of a compliment or some words of hope and support in response to it. Remind students that they need to be very specific in their comments.

4. Write letters. Explain that students are to cut out their selected articles or pictures and then draft a letter to the individuals involved. Their letter should offer a compliment, words of encouragement, or some specific support to the people in the clipping. Offer a concrete example by sharing the "Heartfelt Communication" student sample.

As groups work, circulate among the students and offer suggestions and help as needed. Sometimes they will need concrete ideas to help them get started. They might also need to be guided from using a general statement ("We like what you did") to something more specific ("Helping the couple rake their leaves really showed how much you care").

Give groups clean sheets of writing paper on which to write the final versions of their letters.

5. Mail the letters. Photocopy the letters. Have students mail the originals to the individuals involved in care of the newspaper that ran the story.

6. Create heart displays. After partners have completed their letters, give them red construction paper and have them cut out a large heart and fold it in half. On one half of the heart they will glue their newspaper clipping; on the other half, their photocopied letter.

7. Share the messages. Invite pairs to share their clippings and accompanying messages. A class discussion on the meaning of empathy and caring for others should naturally evolve. Prompt the students to relate this activity to the challenge of bettering the world by asking:

- How does a simple message of hope and caring to people we don't even know help to make the world a more beautiful place?

- Why is it important to reach out to people in this way?

- How does this simple act help to plant "seeds of kindness"?

Incorporate the notion that each of us can easily take relatively cost-free steps to make the world a more beautiful place.

8. Display the hearts. Post the hearts for others to read. Some suggested bulletin board or hallway headings for placement near the hearts are "Heartfelt Messages," "Communicating with a Heart," or "Caring Communications."

For Surefire Success

This activity can easily generate much enthusiasm, especially if you show students your own excitement about the possibilities. Share a letter you have written to encourage someone or to offer a message of hope. If you don't have one to share, describe why the newspaper clippings you selected "caught your heart."

Classroom Extensions

- Challenge students to independently locate another newspaper clipping that elicits the same feelings as those in the activity. Give the students three or four days to locate the news and write an accompanying letter to the individuals involved. Suggest that students mail these letters, too. It might take some effort to locate addresses, but remind students that things worth doing are not always easy. Encourage students to call the local newspaper or library for help, check with the agencies or organizations associated with the story, or look for addresses in the phone book.

- Keep your bulletin board display up for a full term or year and use it to post copies of letters mailed by your students to others. Encourage students to continue to write and post letters throughout the year. If students receive return mail, post this correspondence as well. You might even wish to include a map and use pushpins to mark the locations where correspondents live. Pinning a small heart to a location each time students send a letter will remind your students how many hearts have been touched by their caring.

- Create "good news" of your own. Contact the media and let them know about your project and the results. They might print a story about your class!

School Extension

Encourage other classes (or even the whole school) to join your class in meeting the challenge of making the world a more beautiful place. Why not keep track of the letters mailed from and to students and have a tally at the end of the year? Post a map outside the school office on which students pin a heart for each letter sent. Just think how many lives can be brightened by the efforts of your students!

Heartfelt Communication

Here is a letter written by two sixth-grade students:

May 1, 1996

Dear Dr. Margaret Mies,

We read an article about you in the Daily Times on
April 17, 1996. We were extremely impressed by your
kindness and generosity. We deeply respect your wisdom
in that you know your priorities. The world needs more
doctors like you who don't work for money but for the
joy of service. A surge of happiness rushed through us
both when we read about how you did the cleft lip
surgery at no cost. Even though you didn't do the
surgery for either of us, we can't thank you enough.
We're so glad that Sigi can now lead a normal life. We
think you certainly deserve the honor that will be
bestowed upon you from the National Association of
Women Business Owners. Keep up the great work and don't
ever change your truly magnificent principles!

Sincerely,

Paulo Arriz   *Melanie Vickrey*

Paulo Arriz and Melanie Vickrey

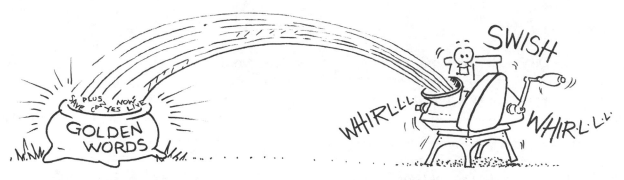

The Rainbow of Words

Popular culture is of interest to many of us, including students. Students want to learn about and emulate a variety of celebrities, from world leaders to sports figures to rock stars. This activity provides a forum for communicating with famous people. In it, students reveal important information about themselves by selecting and explaining five words that describe who they are and what is important to them. Later, they share their thoughts and their work with celebrities from television, movies, sports, business, and politics. If your students need a purpose for writing, this activity is for them! When the writing's done, just sit back and wait for the return mail to arrive.

Learning Objectives

Through this activity, students will:

- think creatively about concrete and abstract concepts
- write their personal thoughts within an assigned framework
- identify personal values, interests, and goals
- identify significant places, things, and people in their lives

Product

Individual rainbows with arcs that tell important personal information about each student's wishes, dreams, and favorite things

Related Curriculum

Language Arts, Social Studies, Art

Materials

- overhead projector and transparency made from "One Student's Rainbow" reproducible master (page 102) *or* copies for each student
- copies of "Rainbow Template" handout (page 103) for each student
- colored pencils, crayons, or markers
- sheet of 8½" x 11" white construction paper for each student
- black fine-line markers
- writing paper
- envelopes and stamps

Optional: The Address Book by Michael Levine

Time

One 45-minute session to make the rainbows; additional at-home or in-school time for students to write letters to celebrities

Preparation

Read through the activity and plan what story you will tell in the introduction (Activity Step 1). Also decide whether you will use your own six words for Activity Step 3. If you will, plan what you will say; make your own rainbow to share as well.

Activity Steps

1. Introduce the activity. You might want to begin this lesson the way we do: with a "Dear Abby" ("Dear Deb," "Dear Jim," "Dear You") story. Feel free to use Deb's, or choose one from your own experience. Ask students: "Who can tell me who 'Dear Abby' is? Who reads her column? What's it about?" Tell students you have a "Dear Abby" kind of story to relate. Here's Deb's story:

A few years ago, a parent from our neighborhood (who knew we were teachers) called to ask for help with her 12-year-old daughter. The mom explained that her daughter was a straight-A student. She was involved in gymnastics three afternoons a week and horseback riding on weekends. She was in Girl Scouts and on the school's swim team.

"My," Deb said to the mother, "your daughter sounds quite talented!"

"That's just the point!" the mom replied. "She's so talented that I want her to do more! Can you give me any advice so that I know what else to do with her in her spare time?"

Here, we ask our students what advice Deb should have given to this mom. They are usually right on target, with comments like, "Tell her to chill out . . . back off . . . get a life!" At this point, we tell students what Deb advised the mother. She put it in the form of a question: "Have you considered letting your daughter catch up on her sleep?" (For the record, this apparently was *not* what the mom was expecting, because she hung up and never called back.)

2. Discuss students' activities. Ask students to share things that they do before school, after school, and on weekends. You'll be amazed at the variety of chores, activities, and social events that occupy the lives of kids so young! They might be surprised, too, if they were to keep track of this on a weekly calendar and add up all of the hours.

3. Describe your approach to "simplifying" your life. Continue this discussion by saying: "Well, I don't know about you, but there are some times when I just want to put my feet up, watch *Gilligan's Island* reruns, and think of life as being a little simpler – maybe even as simple as six little words. In fact, if I could isolate just six words that explained who I was, what I liked, and what my dreams are, here's what they'd be." Reveal the six words you have selected, or use

Deb's words and descriptions:

- Hope – Whether it's a secret desire to win the lottery or a wish to see every country and every kid get along, hope is what makes me believe in a bright future.

- Sand – My favorite memories as a child involve sand – baseball, sandboxes, and the beach. Sand is a word that makes me appreciate the fun of just playing.

- Art – I don't see myself as an artist, but I've always enjoyed looking at art, especially sculpture. Without art, the world would be a pretty blah place.

- Swings – Playgrounds have swings; so do porches and backyards. I've always had a good time on swings, whether alone or with my son. Swings allow me to appreciate my world and my family. They even encourage me to look at the sky in a different way.

- Sunshine – Even the worst problem seems a little easier on a sunny day. With sunshine, I can appreciate the beauty of the sky and the earth at the same time. When I feel warmed by the sun, a smile comes to my face.

- Books – Even before I learned to read, I loved books. I love the way they feel, the pictures inside them, the crackle of the binding when you open a new book for the first time. To me, there is no better gift to give or receive than a book.

4. Discuss the rainbows. If you've made your own rainbow, share it with your students. Also display or distribute "One Student's Rainbow." Point out that everyone in the world – rock stars, athletes, authors, presidents, and students, too – could probably come up with six favorite words. Explain that students will now create their own rainbows and, after sharing them with each other, will share them with a famous (or non-famous) individual of their own choosing.

Ask students to think of someone from television, the movies, sports, the music scene, or the news about whom they'd like to know more and to whom they would like to write.

Optional: To make a real splash with your students, pull out *The Address Book* – a compilation of thousands of addresses of famous people. While students sit there in amazement, say: "Boyz II Men? They're in here. So are Jim Carrey and Mariah Carey and Jesse Jackson and Michael Jordan. Who else would you like to know about?"

5. Create and share rainbows. Ask students to write six words that express who they are and what they like. Suggest that they use scratch paper to write down statements that tell why the words are important to them. Then give students the "Rainbow Template" handout and have them create their rainbows. On each arc, or on the back of the handout, they are to write why they chose these words. Encourage students to illustrate or decorate their rainbows in a way that fits their six ideas. Once completed, students may want to share their rainbows in small groups. A word of caution here: The rainbows can be quite personal; allow students to keep them private if they wish.

6. Mail the rainbows. Invite students to send their rainbows, along with a drawing of a blank rainbow, to the famous person of their choice. Some students might prefer to write to a far-away friend or relative instead. *The Address Book* is a wonderful source for locating many addresses. Libraries, newspapers, CD-ROM sources, and on-line databases would be helpful as well.

Tell students that they are more likely to get a response from someone who is just becoming well known than from a "big name" who may receive thousands of letters each week. Still, our students did hear back from some headliners, including Robin Williams, Whoopi Goldberg, and Reba McEntire. (The best response, though, was a two-page, handwritten note from Susan Butcher. Butcher is an Alaskan woman who won the Iditarod, a wilderness sled-dog race, several times.)

For Surefire Success

- Include a stamped, self-addressed envelope in the letter you send to the famous person. You are much more likely to get a response.

- *The Address Book* is always the most popular book we own – and the one that turns up "missing" the most often. We suggest you buy two copies, and purchase a new copy each year (the book is updated annually). After all, fame changes quickly – today's stars were yesterday's waiters and waitresses!

Classroom Extensions

- When you start to receive completed rainbows from other people, display them and start a "Rainbow Words Collection." You'll be amazed at how similar famous persons' responses are to those of your students.

- Encourage students to write to CEOs of locally based corporations, local politicians or business leaders, older people in the community, and athletes on local teams. The closer to home respondents live, the better the chance of responses.

- Ask students to invite school personnel to complete rainbows, too.

One Student's Rainbow

Here is a rainbow written by a fifth-grade student:

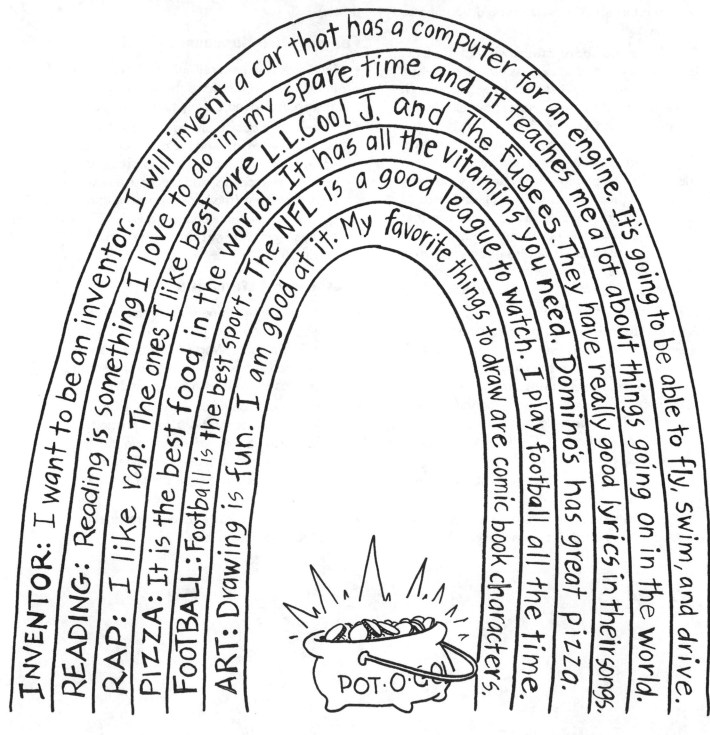

Rainbow Template

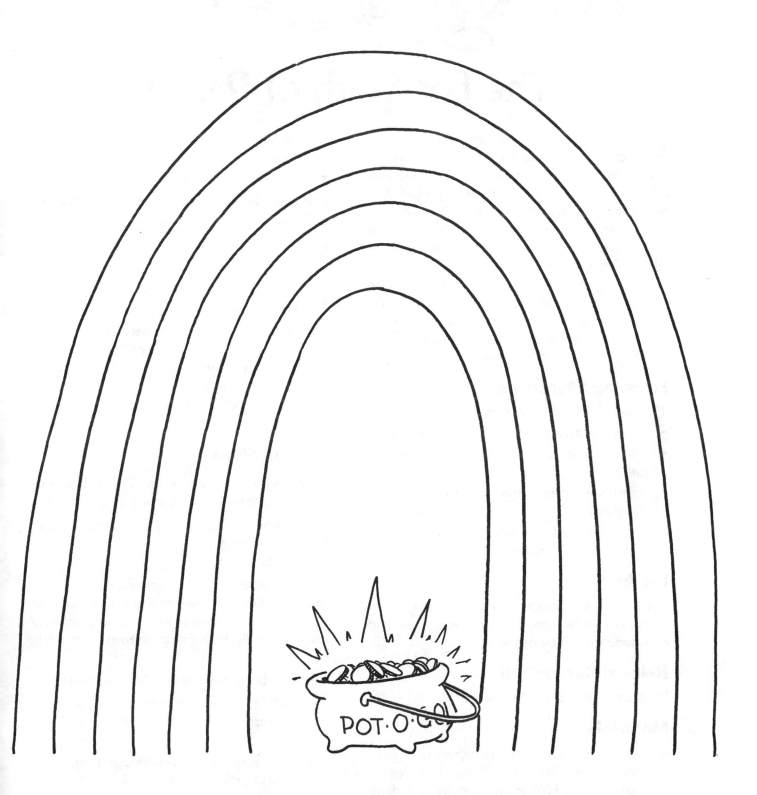

POT·O·G

The Footpath of Peace

With so much violence and anger spewing from our newspapers, televisions, and popular music, it is sometimes hard to believe that our world is filled with more good people than bad, more beauty than bigotry. This activity helps students to recognize that there is much that is positive about our world and, equally important, that each of us can be an agent of peaceful change. Students learn that peaceful change in our world begins with small steps. By hearing about ways that people have chosen to act kindly toward others, students see the benefits of their own kind behaviors.

Learning Objectives

Through this activity, students will:

- recognize that people are interdependent
- identify kindnesses that they have done for others
- identify kindnesses that others have done for them
- write personal accounts about living peacefully and interdependently

Product

Student-created footpath made of students' own footprints emblazoned with messages of kind acts done for and by others

Related Curriculum

Language Arts, Social Studies, Art

Materials

- overhead projector and transparency made from "Footprints of Peace" reproducible master (page 106) *or* copies for each student

- one sheet of construction paper for each student
- pens, crayons, or markers

Optional: Random Acts of Kindness by the editors of Conari Press

Time

One 55-minute session

Preparation

Review the introduction (Activity Step 1). Before the class begins, you may want to write on the board all of the quotations except the one attributed to King. Cover these quotes with a roll-down map or other screen so students won't see them until it is time to discuss them.

Activity Steps

1. Introduce the activity. On the board or overhead projector, write this quote:

"We may have all come on different ships, but we're in the same boat now."
  Dr. Martin Luther King, Jr.

Ask for several interpretations of this quote. Give students a brief overview of King's life. Emphasize his lifelong desire to see change occur peacefully and to have all people be accepted as worthwhile individuals.

Next, write or show these additional quotes:

"It's fearful to know we're connected to everything in the universe, because then we're responsible."
  Glenda Taylor

"The purpose of life is a life with a purpose."
  Robert Byrne

"If there is any kindness I can show, or any good thing I can do to any fellow being, let me do it now, as I shall not pass this way again."
William Penn

"See the squirrel? That's your brother. See the tree? We are related. This is your family; these are all your family."
Brooke Medicine Eagle

"Whenever you are to do a thing, ask yourself how you would act were all the world looking at you, and act accordingly."
Thomas Jefferson

"World peace is us. . . . We are each walking agents of the vision of peace we carry inside us."
Kathleen Vande Keift

Ask for volunteers to state what common idea or sentiment is being expressed by all these people. (You might find it advantageous to have students discuss ideas in small groups or with partners before sharing with the whole class.) It shouldn't take long before one of your students says something like, "All these quotes express the feeling that people have to help each other out," or "Even though each person is an individual, we still have to live together and help each other."

2. Talk about acts of kindness. Remind students that the kind acts people do are not necessarily the things we read about in newspapers and see on the evening news. In fact, kind acts can be in small, everyday actions. Demonstrate this by asking:

- Even though it's a pain, have you or has someone in your family ever returned a shopping cart to its appointed space instead of just leaving it out in the parking lot? Why did you do this? Whom did it help?

- Even if you didn't drop it yourself, did you ever pick up a piece of trash in the school hallway and throw it away properly? Why did you do this? Whom did it help?

- Did you ever send a letter to a teacher or camp counselor or relative to say that the person made a difference in your life? Why did you do this? Whom did it help?

- Did you ever ask an older person to tell you a story about her life – memories of school, how she met her spouse, a favorite song? Why did you do this? Whom did it help?

Tell students that each of the actions they've discussed is a small step toward making the world a kinder place; each of the quotes on the board expresses the belief that even little things can improve our understanding of one another. Explain that students will now share some of their own actions that follow in the footsteps of these others.

Optional: Share with students some of the stories related in *Random Acts of Kindness*.

3. Create footprints for a footpath. Here's where the fun begins. Invite your students to take off one of their shoes and trace the shoe onto a piece of construction paper. On this "footprint," they are to write one act of kindness that they have done for someone else or that someone else has done for them. Display or distribute "Footprints of Peace" and discuss some of the ideas our fourth-grade students included in their footprints.

Encourage students to decorate the footprints as wildly as they like, as long as the writing can be read easily. When the footprints are complete, display them as a footpath along the wall of a school hallway. Point out that, as students walk by this wall, they will see that we are all helping to make the world a kinder place one small step at a time.

For Surefire Success

To ensure an equal number of left and right footprints to display, have students count off (one-two or right-left).

Classroom Extension

There is also a book called *Kids' Random Acts of Kindness*. Have students write their own version of this book by compiling the good thoughts they've written on their footprints.

Footprints of Peace

Here are some students' "footprints of peace":

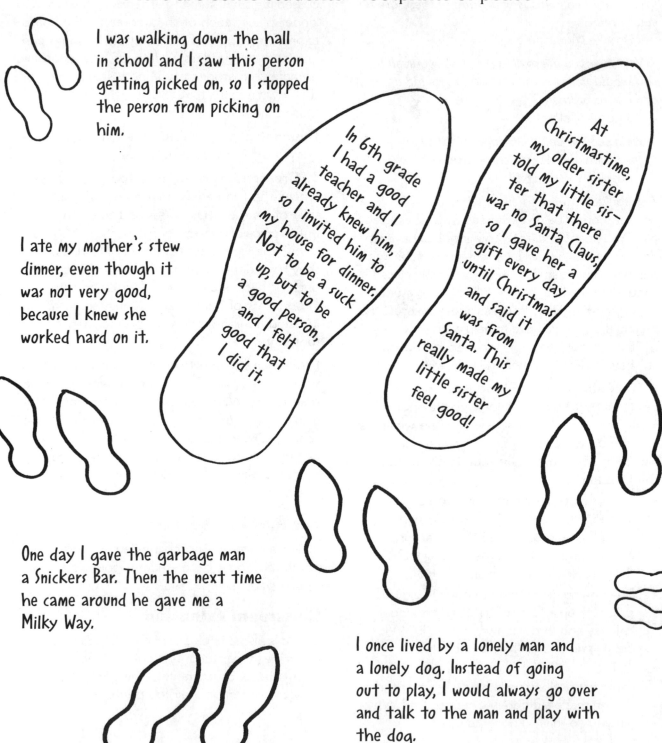

I was walking down the hall in school and I saw this person getting picked on, so I stopped the person from picking on him.

I ate my mother's stew dinner, even though it was not very good, because I knew she worked hard on it.

In 6th grade I had a good teacher and I already knew him, so I invited him to my house for dinner. Not to be a suck up, but to be a good person, and I felt good that I did it.

At Christmastime, my older sister told my little sister that there was no Santa Claus, so I gave her a gift every day until Christmas and said it was from Santa. This really made my little sister feel good!

One day I gave the garbage man a Snickers Bar. Then the next time he came around he gave me a Milky Way.

I once lived by a lonely man and a lonely dog. Instead of going out to play, I would always go over and talk to the man and play with the dog.

"I've learned goldfish don't like Jell-O...!"

Oh, the Things We Have Learned!

Learning is a lifelong process. This activity, in which students interview people of all ages to find what others have learned and are learning, brings this concept home to students in a way they find both interesting and enjoyable. By listening, sharing, and writing about the life lessons of others, students see that every day and every person in their lives is a source of knowledge. They also recognize that life's lessons can be learned by people of all ages – and that their own learning journeys will continue throughout their lives.

Learning Objectives

Through this activity, students will:

- think and work cooperatively on a class project
- ask relevant questions and listen for information
- write about themselves and others within an assigned framework

Product

Student-written class book of "life lessons" in words and pictures

Related Curriculum

Language Arts, Social Studies

Materials

- posterboard or sturdy paper for making three signs
- overhead projector and transparency made from "What I've Learned" reproducible master (page 109) *or* copies for each student
- large index cards (one per student)
- materials for making books (see "Four Ways to Make a Book," pages 33–36)

Optional: Oh, the Places You'll Go! by Dr. Seuss; *Live and Learn and Pass It On* and *Wit and Wisdom from the Peanut Butter Gang* by H. Jackson Brown, Jr.

For School Extensions and Variations: posterboard and pens, crayons, markers, or paints; construction paper, ribbon or string

Time

One 45-minute session; additional at-home or in-school time to complete the activity and assemble the book

Preparation

Read Activity Step 2 and decide whether you wish to interview the three characters we suggest or three others whom you think will be familiar to your group of students. Create three signs labeled "Cinderella," "Abraham Lincoln," and "Shamu," or the names of other characters you've chosen.

Activity Steps

1. Introduce the activity. Gather together all students and say: "Today we are going to meet some fascinating people who have a lot to teach us about ourselves and our world. In fact, these people are cleverly disguised, right now, as some of your classmates."

2. Interview three characters. At this point, invite a volunteer to the front of the class. Then, holding up the "Cinderella" sign for all to see, ask "Cinderella" questions about her life. For example: "What was it like living with your step-sisters?" "How did you first feel when you met the prince?" "How has your life changed since you've moved into the castle?" The last question to Cinderella should be:

• After all these experiences you've had, what have you learned about the goodness and badness of people?

Ask similar questions of other student volunteers portraying Lincoln and Shamu, always ending with the same question.

Then point out to students that many things we learn in life come from the people around us. Explain that, with the help of parents, neighbors, and friends, students will be compiling a book of "life lessons."

3. Share examples of life lessons. Display or distribute "What I've Learned," which shows a page of lessons compiled by children from our classrooms. Read the lessons one by one, asking a volunteer to interpret each. Then tell students that it is now their turn to write some life lessons.

4. Brainstorm ideas in groups. Organize students into cooperative learning groups and assign or let groups choose one of these categories: family, friends, school, myself, our world. Tell students that they are to brainstorm lessons they have learned about their group's category. Allow 5–10 minutes for brainstorming.

Have students share their ideas. You might also read some of the entries from either of the H. Jackson Brown books and ask students to compare their ideas with those of the author.

5. Write life lessons independently. Give every student an index card. Working individually, students are to write three "I've learned that . . ." statements on one side of the index card.

6. Gather more life lessons. For homework, students are to ask family, friends, and neighbors to complete three or more "I've learned that . . ." statements on the back of the index card.

7. Create the book. Once the index cards have been completed, have the students return to their cooperative learning groups. Distribute paper for the book pages and explain that together, group members should select from the combined lists and write 10–20 "I've learned that . . ." statements to be part of a class book.

Optional: To make the point that students have learned a lot and still have many life lessons ahead of them, end the activity by reading *Oh, the Places You'll Go!* Or save this book for the "premiere unveiling" of the class book students have created.

For Surefire Success

Encourage students to ask for "I've learned that . . ." statements from people of varied ages.

School Extensions

• Have some students illustrate the most humorous or meaningful life lessons on large, colorful posters. Hang the posters around the school.

• Compile a bulletin board of lessons learned by teachers, administrators, and school support staff. Place this in a highly visible place in the school.

Variations

• Use this activity as a project for the entire school and compile one large book to be placed in the office or media center for all to enjoy. Or have students trace their hands and write the lessons in the outlines. Display the hands by joining them with ribbon or string.

• Instead of a class book, have students write and illustrate their lessons on 8½" x 11" mini-posters.

What I've Learned

Here are some of the life lessons learned by a group of students and their friends and families:

. . . about family

I've learned that parents can run more miles than kids. — *Age 5*

I've learned that almost all 10-year-olds like to get paid for the things they do. — *Age 64*

. . . about friends

I've learned that a good pal doesn't care what kind of clothes you wear or how messy your hair is. — *Age 11*

I've learned that the most popular kids aren't always the best friends. — *Age 12*

I've learned that a couple of good friends are more important than a thousand casual friends. — *Age 36*

. . . about school

I've learned not to play a big instrument and ride the bus. — *Age 10*

I've learned that short kids sometimes get picked on. — *Age 33*

. . . about myself

I've learned that my name is kind of pretty. — *Age 9*

I've learned that if you put hair spray in your eyebrows they get too stiff. — *Age 11*

I've learned that life is too short to worry about trivia. — *Age 38*

. . . about our world

I've learned that you shouldn't look up into the sun when the teacher tells you not to. — *Age 10*

I've learned that I still have a lot to learn about the earth. — *Age 44*

The Building Blocks of Character

We all have someone in our lives who has influenced us profoundly. In this activity, students select and write about this special person, having first listened to their teachers' recollections of important people in their lives. It's a great activity to do with other teachers and classes with which you intend to do a lot of co-teaching during the year. The person-to-person, teacher-to-student interaction brings up honest human emotions that instill mutual respect almost instantaneously.

Learning Objectives

Through this activity, students will:

- recognize that people are interdependent
- identify significant people in their lives
- identify personal values
- write their personal stories within an assigned framework
- give and accept constructive criticism

Product

Walls of student-created "building blocks" that highlight the character traits of important people in students' lives

Related Curriculum

Language Arts, Social Studies, Art

Materials

- overhead projector and transparency made from "Two Building Blocks" reproducible master (pages 112–113) *or* copies for each student
- copies of "Building Block Template" handout (page 114) for each student, reproduced on various colors of paper

- pens, crayons, or markers
- other decorative art materials
- scissors

Time

One 30-minute session to introduce the activity; additional at-home or in-school time to complete it

Preparation

If you will not be team teaching this lesson with other teachers, arrange ahead of time for at least two colleagues (such as other teachers, the principal, support staff) to share with students their stories about someone important in their lives.

Activity Steps

1. Introduce the activity. In your own words, share the sentiments expressed in the following two paragraphs:

Do you remember who taught you how to tie your shoes? Do you recall who taught you how to read or told you your favorite bedtime story? Can you think of a time when one of your friends or family members was available to listen and help when you were having a really bad day?

Each of us has special people in our lives, people we will always remember, no matter how old we get. These significant people may be young or old, male or female; you may see them every day or only once a year. In other words, each of these important people in your life could be just about anyone.

Tell students that they will be hearing from you and two other school adults about people who have influenced your lives. While you talk, students are to take notes on the characteristics that made the people so important to you. Offer some examples for students to think about: Were the people kind? Helpful? Funny? Patient?

2. Have adults share their stories. With at least two other coworkers, sit in front of your students. One by one, explain who this important person was and what made the person so memorable.

Start by sharing your own story, keeping the length to about 5–8 minutes. Be as specific and personal as you can. When you are finished, allow students to ask you any questions they wish. Repeat this procedure for each panelist.

3. Have students work in small groups. Once the panelists have finished, ask the students to get together in small groups and discuss the specific characteristics they wrote down. Suggest that they also discuss how these characteristics enable people to reach out to others. Allow about 10 minutes.

4. Have students work individually. Ask students to return to their individual places and think of an important person in their own lives who has some of the characteristics they were just discussing. Remind them that this could be a friend, relative, teacher, coach – anyone who has had a personal impact on them. Suggest that they jot down notes about who this person is and why the person has been so special in their lives.

Depending on your time limitation, the next steps could take place immediately or on the following day.

5. Write and revise descriptions. Once students have privately selected an individual who has helped to build their character, have them write a one- or two-paragraph description of why this person was important to them. As they finish, have them discuss the paragraphs with you and with one or two classmates for the purposes of editing. Then students should return to their seats and revise their paragraphs, incorporating suggestions from you and their peers, to make their writing the best it can be.

6. Make building blocks. Display or distribute "Two Building Blocks" and briefly discuss how the students wrote and illustrated the building blocks. Give each student a "Building Block Template" handout. Instruct students to carefully copy their paragraphs onto the blocks. Remind them to be sure their writing can be read easily. Encourage students to add some color and illustrations as well. Such additions really help the individual building blocks to stand out when they are posted on a wall.

7. Build the wall. When the building blocks are completed, post them side by side, creating your classroom's or team's own "Wall of Character."

For Surefire Success

- Be prepared for an emotion-charged adult panel. It's not often that teachers share with students some of their private thoughts about important people in their lives. Still, every time we have done this activity, we have found our students to be polite and respectful of our words and our emotions (spontaneous applause at the end of a panelist's comments is not uncommon). Also, since their teachers take this activity so seriously, students tend to do the same when it is their turn to think and write.

- You may find that many students will write about their parents. Some teachers initially see this as an "easy way out." We suggest you think twice before discouraging children from writing about their parents or caregivers. Many children deeply love and admire the adults with whom they live. Though some children do not live with one or both parents, these adults are still very important in children's lives. It's the students' wall – why not let them build it with any characters they wish?

Variation

If you do this activity with more than two classes, consider erecting several walls of character, each devoted to a different group of people: friends, grandparents, parents, siblings. Discuss ideas for these themes or categories with the students.

Two Building Blocks

Here are two samples based on a fifth- and a sixth-grade student's building blocks:

MY BROTHER

JOSH

My brother is my best friend. We have the best time together. One of the many reasons I admire my brother is he is the best artist in the world! He can draw anything! If I draw something wrong he'll tell me and help me correct it. Sometimes I get mad when he does,tho but I know he's just trying to help me be the best that I can be!

Another reason is he's a very skilled athlete. He is good at football, baseball, basketball, and he can run fast. My brother's abilities are unlimited. That is why I admire my brother.

Building Block Template

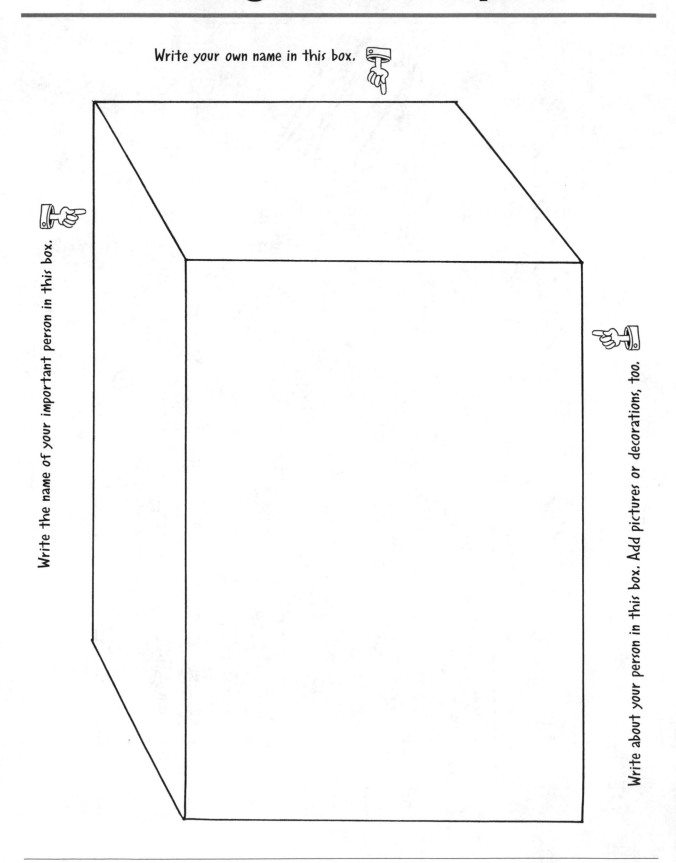

Write your own name in this box.

Write the name of your important person in this box.

Write about your person in this box. Add pictures or decorations, too.

If We Were in Charge of the World

You need to begin this activity with a premise: that most kids believe they can do a better job running the world than do the adults who are now in charge. Here's an activity that gives them a chance to make their point. Using the model of Judith Viorst's well-known poem, "If I Were in Charge of the World," students combine their talents and ideas toward the creation of their own poetic vision of how different life would be if kids were in charge. Because it is generated from the combined efforts of everyone in the class, the final poem reflects at least a bit of each student's contribution.

Learning Objectives

Through this activity, students will:

- identify common problems and common goals
- use individual and small-group ideas to create an original poem
- write their ideas within a standard format

Product

One or more poems that incorporate phrases and sentences created by groups of students

Related Curriculum

Language Arts, Social Studies, Art

Materials

- copies of "If We Were in Charge of the World" handout (page 118) for each student plus, an extra copy for each group of 4–6 students
- scissors
- tape or paste

Optional: *If I Were in Charge of the World and Other Worries* by Judith Viorst

For School Extension: posterboard, fine-line marker, ink pad

Time

One 50-minute session

Preparation

On the board, write these categories: "School," "Brothers and Sisters," "Parents," "Food," "The Environment," "Other Nations or People," "Friends," "Other Things."

Activity Steps

1. Introduce the activity. Begin by asking students if any of them have ever been "the boss" – the person in charge of something. Elicit some specific examples in which students have been leaders (such as captain of a sports team, section leader in choir or band, baby-sitter). Ask students: "What are some of the benefits of being in charge?" (You can expect to hear, "People have to do what I tell them!") Then ask: "What are some of the responsibilities?" ("If things don't turn out right, I'm the one who gets blamed.")

2. Read a poem. Tell your group that you will read what some students would change about the world if they were in charge. Read the poem composed by our students (see "A Sixth-Grade Poem," page 117).

Optional: If you have a copy of the Viorst book, read the poem "If I Were in Charge of the World" to your students.

3. Talk about changing the world. Ask students for ideas about what they would change for each of the categories on the board. Try to gather a few ideas for each category. Write some of the ideas on the board.

Then give students the following challenge: "In small groups, you are each going to brainstorm as many ways as you can think of to change a part of the world."

4. Generate ideas in small groups. Separate students into groups of 4–6 people. Explain that each group is to concentrate on ideas about how they would change one aspect of the world. To encourage truly thoughtful brainstorming, suggest to students that they think of both humorous and serious ideas for improving the world. One student in each group is to serve as a recorder of ideas. Allow about 10–15 minutes for brainstorming.

5. Write lines. Next, keeping students in small groups, distribute copies of the "If We Were in Charge of the World" handout to all students. Ask groups to select the two or three ideas from their brainstorming that they believe are the most creative or important. Explain that they are to take each of these top few ideas and incorporate it into a short phrase or sentence. Encourage students to use the handouts to experiment with different wordings.

When students have refined the wording of their lines, distribute one clean copy of the "If We Were in Charge of the World" handout to each group. Groups may elect to have one student rewrite the lines *or* to cut them out and tape or paste the already-written lines onto the clean handout in the order the group chooses.

6. Create a class poem. This will be your job. Tell students that you are going to take their ideas and put them together into an all-class poem. Collect the groups' finished handouts and use them to compile one or more poems representing the ideas generated by everyone in the class.

For Surefire Success

- Involve as many students as you can in the creation of this poem. (We have used this activity successfully with as many as 110 children simultaneously.) Not only will this give you a greater variety of responses from which to choose, but it will provide a sense of togetherness for an entire class, team, or grade-level group of students. You will also have more poems to create, which should attract much interest.

- Avoid the urge to have each group of students create an entire poem by themselves. If they choose to do so later, that's fine; in fact, it would be great! The purpose here, however, is to combine students' talents toward a common and shared goal: the creation of one poem from the largest number of voices possible. This endeavor adds credence to the notion that we become stronger by working together.

School Extension

Once the poem has been compiled, distribute a copy to each participating student. Ask a friend with good handwriting skills (or, better yet, with a talent in calligraphy) to copy the poem onto posterboard. Have students sign their names, place their thumbprints, or personalize the poem in some other way. One of your students might like to add a creative border or artwork to illustrate the ideas. You might even take a photograph of the authors to include on the poster. Hang this poster near the principal's office – it makes great reading for parents and students waiting to see "The Boss"!

A Sixth-Grade Poem

This poem was composed by sixth-grade students:

If we were in charge of the world,
all drinking fountains would be filled with
  Dr. Pepper,
candy would clean your teeth like toothpaste,
and McDonald's food wouldn't be filled with grease
  or calories.

If we were in charge of the world,
homework would be outlawed,
we'd study from comic books,
and teachers who gave tests would get suspended
  from school.

If we were in charge of the world,
kids couldn't call you names you didn't like,
but if they did, they'd have to kiss and make up with you.

Parents would have to eat brussels sprouts twice
  each week,
and they'd have to go to bed when their kids told
  them to.

If we were in charge of the world,
people who polluted a beautiful place would have to
  pay to build a human-made wonder,
sewers would be replaced with trash-eating plants,
and all the bamboo forests of China would be
  restored.

No hungry or needy people would exist,
every nation would be at peace,
and people everywhere would always understand
  what you are trying to say emotionally,
if we were in charge of the world.

If We Were
in Charge of the World

If we were in charge of the world . . .

_____

_____

_____

_____

_____

_____

_____

_____

_____

_____

_____

_____

_____

_____

_____

_____

_____

_____

_____

. . . if we were in charge of the world.

Shaking Hands with the World

Children care passionately about the future. Bolster students' optimism and tap into their sensitivity by inviting them to offer messages of hope for the future of our world and to share those messages with others in the school. By identifying their wishes for the future of our planet, students begin to recognize the role each person can play as a steward of the earth, an innovative problem solver, and a caring citizen.

Learning Objectives

Through this activity, students will:

- recognize that people are interdependent
- identify personal values, beliefs, and interests
- write their ideas within an assigned framework
- refine their vocabulary

Product

Student-created paper hands, joined together with ribbon or string; each hand offers a wish for the future of our world

Related Curriculum

Language Arts, Social Studies, Art

Materials

- overhead projector and transparency made from "A Sampling of Hands" reproducible master (page 121) *or* copies for each student
- thesauruses
- light-colored construction paper
- pencils
- scissors

- single-hole paper punch
- pens or fine-line markers
- colored pencils, crayons, or markers
- other decorative art materials
- ribbon or string for connecting hands
- tape

Optional: *Kids Share Their Lives through Poetry, Art, and Photography,* edited by Beth Krensky

Time

One 40-minute session; additional at-home and in-school time for decorating and connecting hands for display

Preparation

On the board, draw a birthday cake with candles. (It doesn't have to be "museum ready"!)

Activity Steps

1. Introduce the activity by talking about wishes. Ask students for examples of specific times that they have wished for something. After a few ideas are offered, ask for specific examples of what students might wish for when blowing out the candles on a birthday cake. Write down their ideas on the board around the cake. Most of the responses will identify material goods, such as CDs, new clothes, video games.

Next, change the scenario and ask students what a fictional character having a birthday might wish for. (Use a character well known to your students, such as Barney, Fred Flintstone, E.T., the Wizard of Oz.) Provide a concrete example: "Fred Flintstone might wish for a pair of shoes or a winning lottery ticket." Expand the conversation by including well-known people such as Magic Johnson, the local mayor, or the school superintendent. If you like, list these wishes on the board as well.

2. Share wishes and ideas for a peaceful world. Explain to students that they now must stretch their minds to think about our world and its inhabitants (people and animals) and about the future of our planet. Discuss how each of us can wish for and contribute to world peace.

Optional: Share selections from *Kids Share Their Lives through Poetry, Art, and Photography* with your class. You might also wish to share other books of your choosing about a peaceful future.

Tell students that they will create a display called "Shaking Hands with the World." The display will include cut-out hand tracings with students' ideas for improving our world.

Display or distribute "A Sampling of Hands." Challenge students to think about wishes they might have for our planet, now and in the future. Explain that they are to keep their ideas to themselves. Allow time for students to brainstorm their ideas on scratch paper.

The activity will proceed more smoothly if you help to facilitate students' thinking and writing. Assist individual children to expand their ideas with different word selections, for example. Encourage using a thesaurus for help with descriptive word choices.

3. Create hands. Have each student select a sheet of construction paper. Explain to students that they are to use a pencil to trace their hands onto the paper, then cut out the shapes. Before students begin to write on the hands, have them punch two holes in their paper hands, one at the base of the pinky finger and one at the base of the thumb.

Ask students to write their wishes for our world on their hand cut-outs. Encourage them to be as creative as they'd like, but to use descriptive vocabulary in their writing. They may write on the hands in a variety of ways (for example, one wish per finger, a poem on the palm). Once their writing is complete, have them decorate the hands with designs or small illustrations. Remind students to take care in decorating so that their writing remains easy to read.

4. Connect hands. Weave the hands together using ribbon or string. The ribbon should go through one of the holes, behind the hand, and out through the other hole. Allow 3-4 inches of ribbon between individual hands. A small piece of tape covering the ribbon on the back of each hand will help to keep the ribbon in place.

Hang the connected hands across walls in your classroom, in the hallway, or near the entrance of the school. Decide with your students where the hands will be most effective.

For Surefire Success

You will find that a hallway display is very well received, even if it is created by a single class. Kids love to read the messages on the hands. This might also encourage other classes to join in your parade of hands.

School Extension

Invite other classrooms, or even the whole school, to join your class in this activity.

Global Extension

This activity could easily be expanded to include other schools. Consider having a "hand exchange" with another classroom. If you'd like to connect with a classroom in another part of the country, consider locating one through the "Reader Exchange" column of *Learning Magazine*. Write to *Learning Magazine*, P.O. Box 51972, Boulder, CO 80322. Toll-free telephone: 1-800-334-0298. Or use the Internet or World Wide Web to post an invitation to another classroom anywhere in the world.

A Sampling of Hands

Here are some hands designed by fifth- and seventh-grade students:

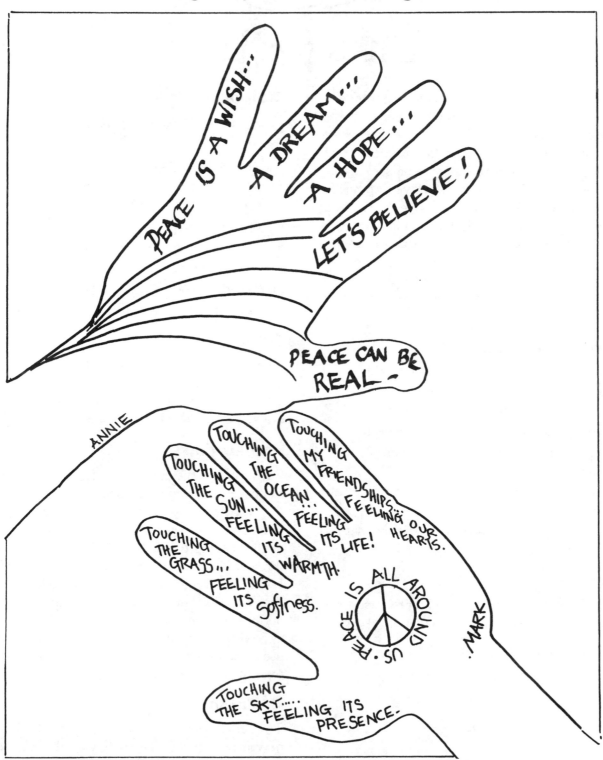

Links for Life

Each person in the world is linked to every other by a bond of common humanity. Here is a schoolwide project that offers a visible way for students to reach out to others and make real links by raising money to support a person, a family, or a cause. This activity, which yields tangible results of students' efforts to make the world a better place, is one that all students in all schools can embrace. Don't be surprised to see even the most "disengaged" students join in with incredible zeal! In this real-world demonstration of students making a difference, the true meaning of charity is realized.

Learning Objectives

Through this activity, students will:
- think and work cooperatively toward a community-centered goal
- recognize that people are interdependent
- consider and set personal and group commitments
- plan and carry out a project over several weeks
- identify individuals and/or situations that prompt empathy

Product

A chain of paper links; each link represents a donation of 10 cents to a particular social cause

Related Curriculum

Social Studies, Art, Language Arts, Math

Materials

- copies of "List of Links" handout (page 126) for each student
- magazines and paper slated for recycling
- scissors
- fine-line markers
- crayons or markers
- other decorative art materials
- stapler or tape

Optional: Every Kid Counts by Margaret Brodkin and the Coleman Advocates

Time

One 30-minute session to introduce and plan the activity; up to two weeks to collect funds for selected charities; additional time to create, decorate, and connect links

Preparation

Read through the entire activity. Create several sample links to show to students.

Apprise yourself of your school's policies and procedures for collecting and tracking money in a fund-raising drive. (See "How to Organize 'Project Person to Person' in Your School," pages 124–125.) Prepare a handout for students and their families that clearly describes these procedures. Plan a time frame for the activity. You may also wish to create a brief script for students to use or adapt when they solicit friends and relatives to purchase links.

Background

The genesis of this activity came in the form of a newspaper article. The story was about a local family in which both parents were killed in separate accidents within a single year. The oldest son, a 20-year-old college junior, would probably need to drop out of school in order to help earn enough money to keep himself and his three younger sisters together. The newspaper story went on to review other devastating losses the parents' deaths had brought about in the surviving children's lives.

Armed with this story and a group of 12 middle-school students who were members of our school's "Project Person to Person" team, we made a collective decision to help this family in a very visible and meaningful way. Specifically, our students decided that we would raise money for this family by creating a chain of paper "links" made from discarded magazines or papers from the recycling bin. Students would sell links, at a cost of 10 cents each, to friends, family members, and other students.

Activity Steps

1. Introduce the activity. With a group of students, visit each classroom in your school and share these true stories of how children have worked to make a difference for other people:

- In riot-ravaged Los Angeles, a class of teens began growing a garden on a city lot. They sold the food they grew at a farmers' market, earning $150. From there, they started a company, Food from the 'Hood, which made salad dressings from the herbs and vegetables the students grew. Now Food from the 'Hood products can be found in grocery stores across Los Angeles. The profits go toward scholarships, tutoring, and family counseling programs.

- In Salt Lake City, a class of fifth and sixth graders lobbied the state legislature and helped pass an environmental cleanup bill that is now a law. They also persuaded the city council to spend $10,000 on badly needed sidewalk repairs and raised $27,000 to plant trees to help with the city's air-pollution problem.

- In Solon, Ohio, a school of fifth and sixth graders donated more than 20,000 food

and household items to local food banks during the holiday season. In addition, this same school's students refurnished an entire household for a family who had lost all their possessions in a house fire.

If you wish, share additional stories of our school's projects related in "Person to Person Projects in Solon, Ohio" (page 125).

Optional: *Every Kid Counts* is a wonderful book to share with your students. It relates many stories of individuals and community groups taking action to make a difference.

2. Discuss efforts that help others. Ask students if they know of any other such efforts led by students (many kids have examples from their girls' or boys' clubs, scout troops, churches, or synagogues). Ask: "Are these efforts worthwhile? Why?" You might want to share the story of our school's experience described in the "Background" section for this activity. Provide examples of your experiences that might fit into this conversation.

Then, by locating people or organizations in your community who need a financial helping hand ("local" sections of newspapers are good sources), have students decide which project they might like to fund. A word of caution: If you are going to assist individuals who, for example, were victims of a fire or similar loss, make sure there is a fund for donations set up through a local bank or charity. This will assure that your students' hard-earned money goes to help the people as intended.

3. Explain the activity. Tell students that in this activity they will "link together," literally and figuratively, the concerns and contributions of many people toward their school's chosen cause. To do this, students will sell "Links for Life." For each 10-cent link purchased, students will write the purchaser's name on a strip of paper, decorate it, and add it to a growing chain of links bought by others. The goal is to have a chain of paper links that encircles the perimeter of the school, weaves through the halls, or enwraps a large common area such as the gym or cafeteria.

Be sure to clearly define fund-raising procedures. Use the materials you created in the "Preparation." Also distribute the "List of Links" handout. Have students write their names on the handout. Take the time to go over procedures step-by-step and to answer any questions students raise.

4. Show how to make the links. Show students the links you have made. Explain how to make them: For each link someone purchases, cut a 1" x 11" strip from an 8½" x 11" magazine page or sheet of paper. Use a fine-line marker to write the donor's name on the link. Decorate it using crayons or markers to create an abstract and colorful design.

Students are to bring the links to class, where they will staple or tape them together with other links to form a long chain.

5. Connect links from all classes. At the end of the link-selling period, arrange to join each class's links to the others. We have each classroom take its connected set of links outdoors (weather permitting) and staple it to the previous class's set. The result is one enormous chain that encircles the entire school (perhaps more than once!) and represents the real money students have collected and put to use for a good cause.

6. Celebrate the school's successful project. Plan and hold an all-school assembly to share the results of your fund-raiser and honor the students' efforts in linking together your hearts and your good ideas. If possible, present the money raised to the recipients themselves or to someone who represents them. Invite the recipients of your donations to address the student body on this occasion.

For Surefire Success

- Part of this lesson can become a math exercise, as students estimate how many links it will take to circle your school. To be accurate, students will need to know the diameter of a link and the perimeter of the school. Talk about hands-on math!

- Be creative in your approaches for getting students involved. We asked our students to give up dessert for one school lunch and buy five links instead, and to create some "Limited Edition Glitter Links" (sprinkled with glue and glitter) that cost 25 cents.

- Send a note home on schoolwide projects, asking families for their support. Many parents offered to take links with them to work as a result of our suggestion.

- Don't allow students to sell links door-to-door. Make it clear that they are to solicit donations from family and friends only. Relatives and friends around the community, the country, and the world can be asked to purchase links.

- Solicit newspaper coverage at both the beginning of this event and at the "closing ceremony." As a result of doing so, we received corporate donations of up to $50 as well as unsolicited donations from people who called our school and asked if they could help out.

How to Organize "Project Person to Person" in Your School

The purpose of "Project Person to Person" is to help locate people or companies in the community who need either students' help or our thanks.

1. Form a committee. Early in the school year, form a "Project Person to Person" Leadership Committee, with one student representative elected from each class, homeroom, or team. The task of this committee is to scour local newspapers to find stories about people close to home who need help or moral support as they are experiencing some especially difficult times. In the process, students may select local companies or individuals who have been especially brave or helpful. To these, your school can send cards or notes of thanks (or, as ours did, a batch of student-made cookies). The committee and its members are to encourage all students in the school to look for people or groups in need of assistance and to relate this information to the Leadership Committee representative from their class.

2. Communicate with all students. Have the student representatives take back to their classmates the stories being discussed and the suggested plans of action. This usually leads to additional suggestions from students.

3. Meet regularly. Schedule a one-hour meeting of the Leadership Committee approximately every two weeks, co-chaired by a student and an adult representative (a teacher, a counselor, an administrator, or a parent). At this meeting, invite committee members to bring up new situations to consider and to discuss appropriate responses, which could range from an individual student writing a note of thanks or encouragement to a schoolwide fund-raising effort. Also use this meeting for an update on any ongoing "Project Person to Person" efforts.

Person to Person Projects in Solon, Ohio

Students sponsored a letter-writing campaign to a man who had a stroke after being hit in the head with a brick thrown through his car window. Each month, a different class sent this man cards, a video of their classroom, and a bouquet of balloons (donated at a child's request by a local grocery). When released from his rehabilitation, the man and his family visited the school to say thank you.

Students wrote thank-you letters to a local toy company, Little Tykes, which had donated more than $17,000 worth of toys to local family shelters and individual recipients. Students sent notes in the shape of their favorite Little Tykes toys. The company president sent back a wonderful note and a collection of other toys for our students to enjoy.

Students collected more than 2,000 stuffed animals, wrote and attached letters, and sent them off to people displaced by a hurricane. The student who thought of this idea stated, "If parents lost their home, then kids lost their toys. This'll give the kids a toy to hug if they're scared."

Students wrote notes of encouragement to a girl who was severely beaten when she told the members of her gang that she wanted to quit. They also wrote letters to the two men who rescued this girl from what would likely have been even more serious injuries or death.

Students sponsored an "All-You-Can-Eat Vegetable Soup Day" in recognition of World Food Day in October. While some students made the soup (with the help of our kitchen staff and parents), others distributed the ceramic soup bowls that were made in their art class. For a $3 donation, diners ate as much soup as they wished; for an additional $3, they could keep the bowl. Community leaders, school board representatives, parents, and others were invited. The students raised more than $700 that day – and took the opportunity to display their recently finished science fair projects, too!

List of Links

Sold by _____

Directions

When you sell any links, write the name of the purchaser, the number of links purchased, and the amount of money you collected.

As soon as you have finished making the purchaser's link(s), place a check mark in the "Links made" column.

Here is an example:

Bonita Suarez	2	.20	X

At the bottom of the sheet, write the total number of links you sold and the total amount of money you collected.

TOTAL SOLD AND COLLECTED			

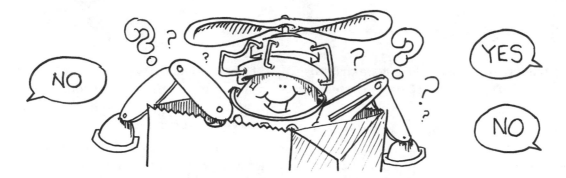

Guess It!

Curiosity is an essential ingredient of human relationships. Through it, we reach out to one another. This activity fosters students' curiosity as it helps them use and refine their higher-level thinking skills. Its implementation is easy: You simply choose objects and invite students to guess what they might be. Your students' task, however, is more complex. Limited to asking "yes" or "no" questions, students are challenged to construct their questions in ways that will yield as much information as possible. In the process, students begin to understand the importance of using precise vocabulary to form concise and specific questions.

This is an ongoing activity that takes little class time. Introduce it early in the school term and keep students guessing all year long!

Learning Objectives

Through this activity, students will:
- think critically
- ask questions to gain information
- use vocabulary in a meaningful way
- develop skills in using language
- derive answers from clues

Product

Student-constructed sets of "yes" and "no" questions that serve as clues in discovering and naming objects

Related Curriculum

Language Arts, Social Studies, Math, Science

Materials

- six coins
- one plain brown shopping bag with handles
- various objects you select (see "Preparation")
- two or more sheets of chart paper or newsprint
- marker
- shoe box
- strong brown paper for covering the box
- scissors or sharp knife
- packaging tape

Time

One 40-minute session to introduce the activity

Preparation

Review the activity and decide how you will display hidden objects so students cannot touch or see them. Consider hanging the bag that holds the objects out of students' reach so they are not tempted to touch or squeeze it (yes, it's very tempting!). Select the first week's object and display it as described in Activity Step 4. Prepare two charts, one labeled "Yes" and the other labeled "No." (You may want to prepare additional charts for use in subsequent weeks.) Wrap the shoe box with brown paper and tape it securely shut. Cut a slit in the top of the box.

Activity Steps

1. Introduce the activity. One fun introduction involves the use of six coins: Tell students that you have six coins in your pocket (jingle them so students can hear). It will be the students' job to figure out what coins you have and what their total value is.

2. Develop questions. Have students work in groups of 3–4 to develop 10 questions that will help them determine the amount of money you have and the value of each coin. Stipulate that you will answer only "yes" or "no" to any question. Stress that students should try to develop questions that will provide them with as much information as possible. (Depending on the age of your students, you may want to challenge them to try to arrive at *five* questions that will lead to the answer. We have had sixth graders accomplish this in four!)

Give an example of a question that yields little information: "Do you have 72 cents?" doesn't help to gain any information at all. "Are all your coins silver?" is a better question; it will eliminate pennies and thus help students take a step toward determining the coins' total value.

WHAT IS IT?

	YES	NO
1. Is it Something to eat?	✓	
2. Is it Something one of us might play with?	✓	
3. Has Dino OR Mark been playing with one like it before class?		✓
4.		
5.		
6.		
7.		
8.		
9.		
10.		

3. Ask questions to solve the problem. After approximately 10 minutes, have the groups ask some of their questions. If students "waste" questions – for example, by asking if there is a specific amount ("Do you have 55 cents?") – stop them and remind them that their questions should be worded in ways that help gather as much information as possible. Try to enhance your students' listening skills by not repeating questions and answers. It's very easy for students to get caught up in their own questions and continually yell out, "What did they ask? I didn't hear it!"

Once a student has solved the problem and guessed the correct amount of money and the value of each coin, ask the student to explain the reasoning behind the solution. Focus on the importance of using specific words and terms to gather information.

4. Explain the ongoing activity. Tell students that they will have an opportunity to develop their questioning strategies. Explain that every week you will display a "What Is It?" bag. Inside you will have placed an object. Students are to guess the contents of the bag by posing a series of questions that can only be answered "yes" or "no." They may ask their questions before or after class. Show students the charts and explain that once you have answered a question, the student is to write the question on the appropriate chart.

Remind students that as the week progresses they will need to review the questions already asked and posted on the charts. These questions will help them refine their own thinking. Once someone knows the answer, that student is to write the answer and the date and time of the guess on a slip of paper, sign it, and place the paper in the shoe box. It is up to you to decide if students can make more than one guess.

Tell students that at the end of the week you will look through the papers in the box to see if anyone arrived at the correct response. If more than one student guessed correctly, you'll check the dates and times to see who guessed first. You will also review the questions asked and discuss how students developed their thinking in order to figure out the correct answer.

For Surefire Success

- Initially, you may have to interject some questions of your own in order to spur students' thinking.

- Consider using objects that students may keep if they guess correctly, such as a small bag of candy or even an object from the infamous "junk drawer."

- To open the box, run a knife under the edge of the cover. Use strong packaging tape to reseal the box.

The Great Idiom Contest

You've seen them and you've loved them. You've scratched your head over their solutions only to see the obvious once the answers were revealed to you. Newspapers and magazines include them as a regular feature; bookstores stock whole volumes devoted to them. What is it about word puzzles that sparks our interest?

Here's an activity that lets you pass on the fun of playing with language to students by challenging them to create "visual idioms," word puzzles for classmates to solve. At the same time, students will explore the hundreds of idioms that are part of the English language. If your class includes students whose first language is not English, there will be the added bonus of an introduction to the idioms of another language. Conduct the activity with a single class or use it to set up a little friendly competition between classes.

Learning Objectives

Through this activity, students will:
- analyze phrases and word usage
- think and work cooperatively
- communicate within an assigned framework
- expand their vocabulary and facility with language

Product

Student-generated visual word puzzles representing idiomatic language

Related Curriculum

Language Arts, Art, Math

Materials

- abridged idiom dictionaries appropriate for students (see "For Surefire Success," page 132) *or* your own prepared list of idioms (see "Preparation")
- overhead projector and transparencies made from "A Sad (but True) Tale" reproducible master (pages 133–135) *or* copies for each student

Optional: *Mad As a Wet Hen! And Other Funny Idioms* by Marvin Terban; *Plexers* and *More Plexers* by Dave Hammond

Time

Two 45-minute sessions

Preparation

Review the activity steps. Decide whether to conduct the activity within a single class or between two classes. If you divide a single class, plan a way for each team's small groups to work out of sight and earshot of the others.

If you do not have enough abridged idiom dictionaries for each small group, compile your own list, making it as long as possible.

Activity Steps

1. Introduce the activity. On the board, write some rebus word puzzles that represent idioms such as these:

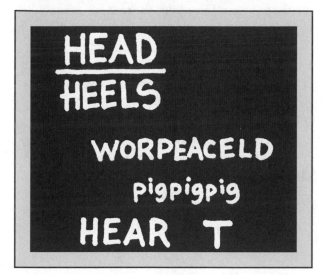

Ask for interpretations from the students. (These represent "head over heels," "peace in the world," "three little pigs," and "broken heart.") Then ask for volunteers to draw their own word pictures on the board.

2. Talk about idioms. Ask students: "Who can tell us what an idiom is?" Accept answers and discussion until you are sure all students understand the concept:

- An idiom is a phrase or expression that has its own unique meaning. The meaning goes beyond the individual words themselves – in fact, if you define the words one at a time, then string the definitions together, the phrase doesn't make sense! Each language has its own idioms, and idioms can't be translated from one language into another.

Hold up an idiom dictionary or your prepared list and, if you have it, *Mad As a Wet Hen! And Other Funny Idioms*. Read some examples:

- the long and the short of it
- an open and shut case
- fit for a king
- on top of the world
- in a nutshell.

Ask students what each phrase means. Then ask if they can think of any ways to visually represent these phrases.

Display or distribute "A Sad (but True) Tale" and ask students to interpret the rebus pictures. (Wait to share the solutions, which are on the last page of the reproducible master, until students have a chance to read through the story.) Within no time, you'll have the students primed for the group activity: "The Great Idiom Contest."

3. Explain the contest. Tell students that there will be two large teams (the two halves of the class or two classes). Explain that teams will break into small groups to brainstorm idioms and other phrases and create visual puzzles representing the phrases. Teams will then attempt to solve one another's word puzzles.

4. Create word puzzles. Divide students into two teams. Have each team's members break up into smaller work groups of three students. Give each small group an idiom dictionary or your prepared sheet of idioms. Tell groups that they are to brainstorm as many different idiomatic phrases as possible. In addition, they may use some phrases or words that are not idioms, but that can be displayed visually (such as "three little pigs"). Have the students write and draw as many visual idioms as they can within an allotted time period (we suggest at least 20 minutes). At the end of this step, each group is to turn in to you their visual idioms and solutions.

5. Compile each team's word puzzles. Either alone or with the help of a colleague or friend, compile each team's puzzles onto one page. If you feel creative, turn the puzzles into a story as we've done in "A Sad (but True) Tale." Compile solutions on a separate sheet.

6. Hold an idiom contest. The next day, or as soon as possible, combine the two teams or classes. Once again, divide teams into small groups of three, giving each group an idiom dictionary and a copy of the other team's visual word puzzles. Then, with the help of their logic and their dictionaries, students will have 20 minutes to try to decipher the other team's puzzles.

The team that correctly solves the most puzzles is declared the:

WINNER

(You guessed it – the "big winner"!)

For Surefire Success

- Don't be too strict with your interpretation of idioms, at least not initially. Let the students create word pictures to get them used to the idea that words and phrases can be expressed in numerous ways.

- A word of warning: Most idiom dictionaries we've seen in schools are unabridged. A safer bet for younger eyes is the *Mad As a Wet Hen!* book (and its follow-up books by the same author).

Classroom Extensions

- As a wonderfully creative follow-up to this lesson, have interested students take their visual idioms and word pictures and turn them into a fairy tale, short story, or tall tale. "A Sad (but True) Tale," created by a group of students and their teacher, made the rounds in our teachers' lounges and was included in a monthly parent newsletter – a good reminder that language can be as much fun as you want it to be.

- Once your students get hooked, put one visual idiom on the board at the start of each day. *Plexers* or *More Plexers* will provide enough examples for the entire school year. Many newspapers also run daily rebus puzzles such as "Wuzzles" by Tom Underwood.

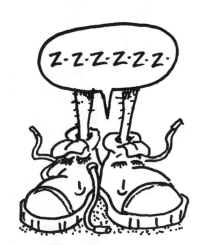

A Sad (but True) Tale

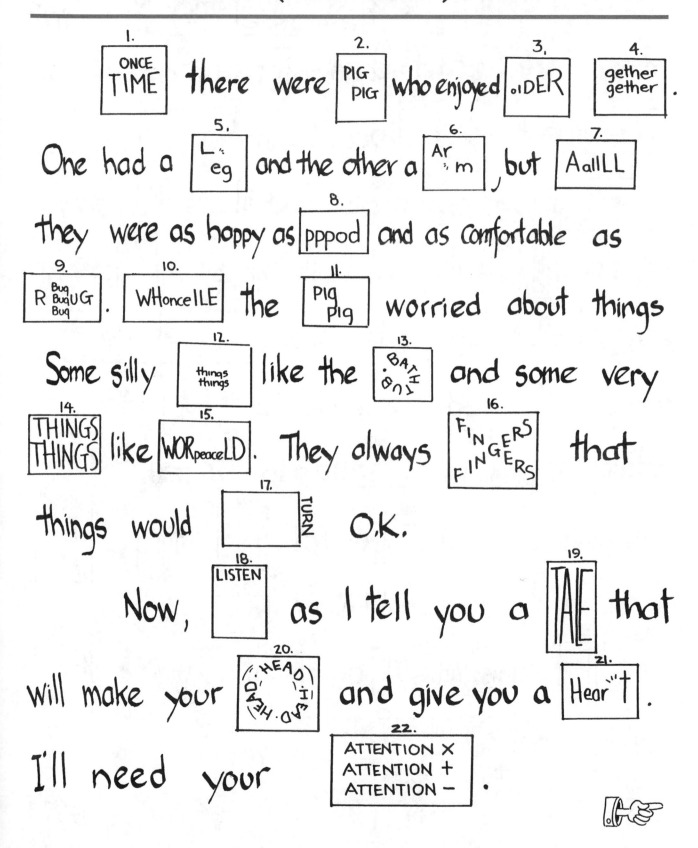

Since the pigs were [**23.** PSSSSSSSSSSSS' BROKE] they needed some money. They hoped to earn [**24.** fi$$$st] in order to make [**25.** endsends], but their [**26.** SACKS WALL BACKS] because they were [**27.** School] [**28.** DROP DROP] !

[**29.** NUT in SHELL], the pigs couldn't even read. That's how they got into [**30.** TROUBLE]. They jumped into their car, a [**31.** BEAT] chevy, with [**32.** 4]. After they [**33.** Buckled], they took a [**34.** DRIVE] [**35.** COUN in TRY], hoping to find work that would help to put [**36.** food TABLE].

Instead, the pigs went [**37.** PAST] a sign that read [**38.** Construction ROAD].

They ended up going [**39.** head heels] over the [**40.** MOUNTAIN], hitting a [**41.** WAITER] on the [**42.** WAY]. It was so sad I almost [**43.** cried eyes] !

[**44.** IT IT] is this: [**45.** SCH stay OOL] or else it's [**46.** Strike Strike Strike YOU'RE] in the ol' ball game. [**47.** THE]

Solutions to "A Sad (but True) Tale"

1. Once upon a time
2. two little pigs
3. growing older
4. together
5. broken leg
6. broken arm
7. all in all
8. two peas in a pod
9. three bugs in a rug
10. Once in awhile
11. two little pigs
12. little things
13. bathtub ring
14. big things
15. peace in the world
16. crossed their fingers
17. turn out
18. listen up
19. tall tale
20. head spin
21. broken heart
22. undivided attention
23. flat broke
24. fistfuls of dollars
25. ends meet
26. backs were against the wall
27. high school
28. dropouts
29. In a nutshell
30. big trouble
31. beat-up
32. four on the floor
33. buckled up
34. long drive
35. in the country
36. food on the table
37. right past
38. road under construction
39. head over heels
40. mountainside
41. waterfall
42. way down
43. cried my eyes out
44. The long and the short of it
45. stay in school
46. 1, 2, 3 strikes you're out
47. The end

Creative Inventors

Here's an opportunity to teach creative problem solving with a touch of whimsy. Working cooperatively, students will invent a method or machine that solves a problem you present. Though humor will play a part in students' conceptions and designs, the larger lesson, that people can work together to the benefit of others, will not be lost.

Learning Objectives

Through this activity, students will:

- work and think cooperatively and creatively
- think spatially
- represent three-dimensional objects in a two-dimensional format
- explain their ideas orally and in writing
- recognize that there are many ways to accomplish a single goal

Product

Student-conceived and drawn plans and explanations for inventions

Related Curriculum

Language Arts, Social Studies, Science, Math, Art

Materials

- copies of "Inventive Brainstorming" and "Our Invention: How Will It Work?" handouts (pages 138–139) for each group of 2–3 students
- plenty of unlined paper
- chart paper or posterboard (one sheet for each group of students)
- pencils

- pens, colored pencils, or markers
- large index cards (one for each group of students)

Optional: The Wizard of Oz by L. Frank Baum (book or video – see "Preparation")

Time

One or two 40-minute sessions; additional time for oral presentations

Preparation

Review the story of The Wizard of Oz, paying attention to how Dorothy is removed from Oz and finally returned to Kansas.

Activity Steps

1. Introduce the activity. Begin by reviewing with students the story of The Wizard of Oz. Ask students to explain how Dorothy eventually returned to Kansas from Oz.

Divide students into groups of 2–3. (More than three generally makes this activity cumbersome.) Explain that the groups have been hired by the Wizard of Oz to invent a creative new way to return Dorothy to her home in Kansas.

2. Conceive inventions. Distribute copies of the "Inventive Brainstorming" handout and ask the groups to generate, through brainstorming, a list of 20 possible ways to get Dorothy home. Challenge students to be creative and original in their ideas. Have a recorder from each group list the ideas on a sheet of paper. When they've finished brainstorming, groups are to mark with an asterisk (*) the three ideas that represent their best, most creative thinking.

Allow an opportunity for every group to share their ideas with you. You might tell them that you are the "Wizard's Wonder," second in command to the Wizard himself! Help each group select one idea to pursue or have the other class members help to decide.

Give each group a copy of the "Our Invention: How Will It Work?" handout. Explain that students are to discuss the ideas on the handout in preparation for drafting designs of their inventions.

3. Draft designs. Once the decision has been made and discussed, have each group draft the design for their invention on a blank sheet of paper. Again, have students share their initial draft with you. Check to be sure that they have included enough details so that others will recognize how their contraption works.

4. Finalize designs. Once the rough drafts are finalized, have groups produce designs for their inventions on large, unlined sheets of chart paper or posterboard. Students should work in pencil first, then use pens, markers, or colored pencils to complete their designs. Remind students to include a name for their group's invention on the final design.

5. Write explanations. Have each group draft and finalize an explanation of how their invention works. Each group is to write the final version on an index card and attach it to their poster.

6. Share designs. After all groups have completed their work, each group should present and explain its invention to the class.

For Surefire Success

- Monitor groups closely and encourage students to stretch their original ideas or to combine some of their ideas into one.

- To help students get started, provide a "far-out" example, such as a giant rubber band used as a slingshot.

- Prior to listening to the groups' presentations, you might want to think about some clever awards ("Zaniest Idea," "Most Expensive Idea") you can present to different groups for their completed masterpieces. As the "Wizard's Wonder," present the awards after all presentations have been made.

Inventive Brainstorming

You have been hired by the Wizard of Oz to invent a creative new way to return Dorothy to her home in Kansas. Start by brainstorming 20 ideas. When you've finished, select the three best ideas. Mark those three with an asterisk (*):

1.

2.

3.

4.

5.

6.

7.

8.

9.

10.

11.

12.

13.

14.

15.

16.

17.

18.

19.

20.

Our Invention: How Will It Work?

Before you design your invention, think and talk about how it will work. Use this sheet to help your thinking and planning:

What will we call our invention?

What will it do?

What materials will be used to make it?

How will it work?

What could go wrong? How can we prevent that?

How can we draw a plan for it?

Building a Book Report

Need an idea for a hands-on activity that fuses language arts and math skills? Here's a project that will surely entice every student. First, students explore different reading genres and identify one that they particularly enjoy. Then they read and discuss their books with other students who are reading in the same genre. Students then go on to design and build a three-dimensional structure that represents their genre and displays their book reports.

This activity can be designed and carried out in a variety of ways, depending upon the age of your students, your curriculum needs, and your instructional style. The overall intent is for your students to become actively involved in "building" book reports. As they do, they'll gain valuable experience in conceiving, planning, and carrying out a team project.

Learning Objectives

Through this activity, students will:

- think creatively
- work and think cooperatively
- plan and carry out a project over several weeks
- symbolize both abstract and concrete ideas
- represent three-dimensional objects in a two-dimensional format
- plan and build three-dimensional structures
- write within an assigned framework

Product

Student-created structures representing specific book genres and displaying summaries of students' reading

Related Curriculum

Language Arts, Math, Art

Materials

- library books representing a variety of genres, such as mystery, science fiction, historical novel, biography
- copies of "A Plan to Build Our Book Report" handout (pages 142–143) for each group of 4–6 students
- plenty of chart or graph paper
- markers
- materials for building and decorating such as posterboard, cardboard, construction paper, rulers, tape measures, scissors, glue, and paints (make this as simple or elaborate as you wish)

Time

One 40-minute session to introduce the activity; additional in-school time to build models; one or two additional 40-minute sessions for sharing models

Preparation

Review the activity and decide how to help groups select genres. Be prepared to help students find different books in their assigned genres, so that no title is read by more than one student.

Activity Steps

1. Introduce the activity. Discuss the term "genre" and the different genres of books. Help students identify their favorite genres by asking about the types of books they like to read. Use different library books to show examples of different genres. Tell students that they will be exploring one genre by reading in it, talking and writing about it, and building an object that represents it.

2. Organize students into small groups. Explain that everyone in a given group of 4–6 students is to choose and read a book in one genre. Have or help students select the books they will read. It is important that titles not be duplicated.

3. Read books. Allow a reasonable amount of time for students to read the books they have selected.

4. Discuss books in small groups. Following the completion of the reading, have groups reconvene to discuss their books. After talking about individual books, groups are to focus on the genre itself: For example, what are characteristics of this genre? They should write their ideas on large chart paper.

5. Explain the project. Explain that each group's task will be to select a three-dimensional object that will represent their designated genre and to build that object. Discuss the meaning of "three-dimensional"; ask for examples (such as a dollhouse or LEGO structure). Make certain that students understand what it means to "represent" the genre. Offer some examples:

- Students might design and build an eerie mansion to represent the genre of mystery. A summary of each of the books read by group members might appear in the windows of the house.

- A group might create a 4-foot rocket to illustrate science fiction. Each rocket stage could represent one of the individual books read by group members.

Part of the students' task will be to incorporate the summaries of their books into the object they construct.

6. Decide what to build. Depending upon the grade level of your students, you might wish to facilitate the discussions of each group. Encourage students to think creatively about how best to represent their genre.

7. Draft designs and plan the building process. After they have decided upon their desired object, have students draft a design on a sheet of chart or graph paper. Be sure that they have included a place for each of the summaries of their books. Then have them list what materials they will need and who will be responsible for securing materials (other than those you are willing to supply). Give students copies of "A Plan to Build Our Book Report." Help groups develop a plan that includes a time line.

8. Build. After the students have completed their plans, the next challenge will be for them to construct the models.

9. Share the models. Once all of the groups have completed their projects, take time for students to share their models and summaries with one another.

For Surefire Success

- Allowing classroom time to complete the projects will energize your groups. You can better encourage the students to think creatively and to stretch their limits if this project is completed in school.

- Encourage students to help one another locate materials from home to complete their projects, such as an old dollhouse that can be transformed into a mystery mansion.

- This is a wonderful activity for teaming with your school's media specialist.

Classroom Extension

You can easily adapt this project to other content areas. For example, students might build a structure to highlight their study of history: an Inuit snowhouse or a Navajo hogan, an Egyptian mummy case, a medieval castle, a "Great Wall," a pyramid, a covered wagon. The entire class can work together on one model to display all the reading summaries.

Variation

Have the entire class focus on one specific genre, with each group reading different books within that genre.

A Plan to Build Our Book Report

Write a description of what you plan to build here: _____

_____

_____

_____

What materials will you need? Where will you get them? List the materials here:

What are the tasks that need to be done? Which comes first, second, and so on?
When does each task need to be done? Write the tasks in order here:

1.		
2.		
3.		
4.		
5.		
6.		
7.		
8.		

Create a time line for completing your project here:

Games to Go

Most children are familiar with a variety of board games. Channel this interest and challenge your students to a truly comprehensive project: conceptualizing and creating their own board games. Throughout the many weeks they spend developing, testing, and refining their games, students will stretch their skills in cooperation and problem solving to new limits. And you will marvel at the level of originality many student groups are able to conceive and sustain.

Adapt the activity to fit any content area. Whatever the subject – geography, literature, biology, foreign language, or mathematics – this game-making project will breathe new life into it for both you and your students.

Learning Objectives

Through this activity, students will:
- learn the format of game boards
- work and think cooperatively to design a board game
- plan and carry out a project over several weeks
- think spatially
- give and receive constructive criticism
- write directions within a standard format

Product

Student-created board games

Related Curriculum

Social Studies, Language Arts, Math, Art

Materials

- several different board games, including some that are linear (such as Candyland) and some that are cyclical (such as Monopoly or Life)
- plenty of chart paper or newsprint
- tape
- copies of "Game Plan" handout (pages 148–149) for each group of four students
- materials for making games (see "What's in a Game?" page 147)
- copies of "Playing the Game" handout (page 150) for each field test group

Optional: TNT Teaching: Over 200 Dynamite Ways to Make Your Classroom Come Alive by Randy Moberg

Time

Six to eight 40-minute sessions (most of this time is independent, but monitored, group work; some at-home or independent in-school time might be substituted for class time)

Preparation

Determine the game-making topic and any specific criteria students will need to meet. For example, if the game is to be related to a science unit on the rain forest, decide what aspects of this study you will require students to include.

To ensure that all students are familiar with some board games, you might want to have several available in the classroom and allow small groups to use class time to play and analyze the games.

You may wish to prepare charts for the discussion of linear and cyclical games (see Activity Step 1).

If you have a copy of *TNT Teaching: Over 200 Dynamite Ways to Make Your Classroom Come Alive*, familiarize yourself with the "Design-a-Game Kit" on pages 137–46. This information can be of great help to you and your students as they proceed with this activity.

Activity Steps

1. Introduce the activity. Ask students what their favorite board games are. List the games on the board.

Divide students into groups of four and assign each group one of the games listed. Ask groups to determine how the game is designed. Tell them to first focus on the board itself and to describe the pathway each player must follow. Next, have them analyze the game's directions. Be sure students understand that the directions are written in a sequential, detailed format. Have groups share what they've discovered with the class. You may want to chart the group's explanations so that students can have a visual representation of the similarities and differences among the games.

Introduce students to the two basic formats of games: linear and cyclical. Linear games, like Candyland, involve moving a token from start to finish as quickly as possible. Cyclical games, like Monopoly, involve moving a token around and around one pattern and acquiring property or some other predetermined set of goods.

2. Explain the activity. Challenge groups to develop a game of their own. Clearly define the topic and any other criteria you have established. Explain that each group will:

    A. Brainstorm game ideas

    B. Plan the type, design, and parts of the game

    C. Review and critique one another's plans as a way of troubleshooting and gathering additional ideas

    D. Create a mock-up and revise plans

    E. Construct the game and write directions

    F. Field test the game

    G. Revise the game to improve it and correct problems discovered in field testing

    H. Package the game.

3. Conduct the activity. Proceed with the activity tasks:

Task A: Brainstorm

Encourage groups to start by thinking about the object of their game. Explain that, in selecting the specific type of game they will make, each group must decide whether their ideas will best fit into a cyclical or linear format. For example, if the game is to be based on a novel, the object might be to have a main character travel along a path of the story's settings and acquire items such as money, experiences, and clues. Or, the game's tokens could represent main characters who need to get to a final destination as quickly as possible. Remind students that they need to decide this first and must be able to explain their rationale for selecting a cyclical or linear format.

Task B: Plan the game

The most difficult task begins after groups have chosen the type of game they will make. To facilitate this essential planning step, give students the "Game Plan" handout and go over it with them. Have each group tape a large sheet of chart paper to a table or the floor. This will serve as their planning map. As the group's members brainstorm ideas, one student should record the ideas on the chart paper. After brainstorming, have the groups share their general ideas with the class. Encourage helpful comments and suggestions.

Next, have students categorize their ideas into specific topics: rules, playing pieces, board design. Explain that once the ideas are categorized, it will be easier for students to discuss and determine which ideas will work best.

Task C: Review and critique plans

After each group reaches a consensus about the design of their game, have them work with another group to review their plans. The essential question for each group to ask is: "What will happen if _____?" To demonstrate the type of critiquing groups should conduct, provide a specific example, such as: "What will happen if a player lands on a 'Challenge' square?"

Task D: Create mock-ups

Using sheets of scrap paper or cardboard, have each group make a mock-up of their game. They may use symbolic representations and labels just to get their ideas down. This is a critical step because the students need to see a visual representation of their ideas. Often, their ideas don't correspond with what they think the game will look like. By looking carefully at the drafted design, students will be better able to evaluate whether the decisions they've made about such issues as how a player advances or how cards are used with directions will actually work. They may discover additional ideas, such as adding penalties or rewards for landing on specific spaces.

The mock-up also provides groups with a chance to revisit the original intent of the project. For example, if the game is supposed to be tied to a specific topic, they'll need to decide if their plans include enough appropriate vocabulary and concept development. Counsel students not to make their games too complex; otherwise they run the risk of losing the interest of their audience.

Task E: Construct the game

Now it's down to the basics: actually constructing the gameboard and the playing pieces. Encourage students to work with a variety of materials; suggest that posterboard, construction paper, and plastic pieces work well. They'll also need to consider the visual effect of their game: Is it attractive?

After assembling the game, the group will need to decide upon and write complete, precise directions. Remind students to proofread and edit all of their writing carefully. They'll want to check their spelling and grammar as well as the clarity of their directions. Also stress to students that, while *they* might be certain of how the game should progress, the players will come to the game without benefit of the group's thinking. Have students look at the format of directions of other games. As groups write directions, stress the need for clarity and explicitness.

Task F: Field test the game

Once the games are completed, arrange a time for the groups to field test their games. You may elect to do this with the groups who have actually worked on the project or to enlist students from other classes who are unfamiliar with the project. Have field testers use the "Playing the Game" handout to structure their evaluations.

For field testers, stress that their contribution is not based on who wins the game, but rather on providing the game creators with helpful suggestions that will make the games more interesting or the directions easier to understand. Both you and the game-making groups should listen to how the field testers explain the rules and progress around the board. Remind game designers not to interrupt the players with explanations. If the game needs to be explained, that is a clear indication that the design or instructions need to be fine-tuned.

Task G: Revise the game

Have the groups make changes based upon the field testing. Sit with individual groups to discuss their progress.

Task H: Package the game

Encourage groups to be creative in their packaging ideas. Urge them to consider other options besides traditional boxes. Have cardboard and other materials available for packaging. Remind students that it is best to be "earth-friendly" and recycle some materials; for example, students can turn an old laundry soap box into a game box. Be sure that the containers students use are sturdy.

4. Enjoy the games! Keep the games prominently displayed and available in the classroom. Remind students to treat the games carefully as they play and put them away.

For Surefire Success

- This is a great activity for involving parent volunteers. It is often difficult, although not impossible, to circulate among all of the groups and to provide as much help as might be required. Even one extra pair of helping hands is a welcome addition.

- Consider teaching a mini-lesson on the writing of directions. Simply use the directions from a game to demonstrate how words are used to be precise. Explain to students that, in writing directions, nothing should be assumed about the players' knowledge or understanding of how the game is played.

Classroom Extensions

- Have an interested student or group of students write to game manufacturers to request information about how the companies select games. Consider submitting one or two of your class's games for these companies' consideration.

- Have students research games of different cultures and create games based on the different formats they discover.

School Extension

Invite other classes to make games as well. Then hold an all-school "Games Fair." Feature games and game playing, add refreshments and prizes, and appoint a panel of judges. Invite families and others in the community to attend the event.

Community Extension

This activity easily lends itself to a community project. Perhaps your students could design games for a local preschool or children's ward of a hospital.

What's in a Game?

Games can be constructed from the simplest to the most elaborate materials. If possible, have on hand a range of materials. Suggest additional materials students may wish to locate for themselves. Here is a good starter list:

- pencils and erasers
- rulers and yardsticks
- tracing paper or carbon paper
- scissors
- scrap paper or cardboard
- illustration board, foam core, or precut plywood
- glue or rubber cement
- ballpoint pens or fine-line markers
- permanent markers or paints
- paper clips, straight pins, pushpins, brads
- stencils or stick-on letters
- construction paper
- clear adhesive paper or laminating material
- miscellaneous small objects such as old game pieces, foam core scraps, and bottle caps

Game Plan

Things to consider

- game type (linear or cyclical)
- object of game
- rules
- playing pieces
- tricks
- board design
- scoring

Questions to discuss

1. For what ages is the game intended?

2. What should be the starting point?

3. What might be the finishing point?

4. What is the object of the game?

5. Is the game competitive? How is the winner determined?

6. How many people can play (minimum and maximum)?

7. What is the suggested playing time?

8. What barriers might the players encounter?

9. How do the players move forward?

10. If the game will have cards or a spinner, what will be on those items?

11. Will there be penalties or rewards for landing on certain spaces?

Playing the Game

As a game field tester, you have a very important job. You need to let the game makers know what happens when you play the game. Use this sheet to write your comments.

1. Are the directions written clearly? If not, what do you <u>not</u> understand?

_____

_____

_____

2. Does the game work like the directions say it will? If not, what *didn't* work? How do you think the game makers could fix this problem?

_____

_____

_____

3. Is the game   ❏ too long?   ❏ too short?   ❏ just right?

4. What do you like best about this game? _____

_____

_____

_____

5. What other comments or ideas do you have for the game makers?

_____

_____

_____

The Kaleidoscope of Culture

Regardless of who they are or where they live, our students can't help but be aware that our society includes people of different cultures. Using the wonderful examples from Norine Dresser's *I Felt Like I Was from Another Planet*, introduce your students to some of the small cultural differences that can lead to big misunderstandings. Through a role play that presents some cultural norms different from their own, students come to realize the importance of understanding an individual's behavior and the foolishness and cruelty of ridiculing anyone for what only *seem* like "strange habits."

Learning Objectives

Through this activity, students will:

- recognize similarities and differences among cultures
- recognize that there is more to people than what we see on the surface
- appreciate and value differences
- empathize with others

Product

Posters, brochures, skits, puppet plays, or other mediums students choose for sharing with others what they learn about cultures and cultural differences

Related Curriculum

Social Studies, Language Arts, Art

Materials

- two natural objects (such as seashells, tree bark, or abandoned birds' nests) from two different geographic places
- bathrobe or pajamas
- three soup spoons and bowls
- three small musical instruments (or other things that make sounds)

Optional: I Felt Like I Was from Another Planet by Norine Dresser

Time

One 50-minute session to introduce the activity; additional at-home and in-school time to complete selected products

Preparation

Review Activity Step 3, part of which involves playing musical instruments. Ask two students to help you out by being the "plants" – one who shouts joyously and one who tells the other to leave the "concert."

Activity Steps

1. Introduce the activity. Begin by showing students the two natural objects you've selected. We show our students two conch shells, one found in South Carolina and the other from the New Zealand coast. Without mentioning their geographic origins, we ask students to find ways that the two shells are similar to and different from each other.

After several comparisons, we ask for a show of hands: "How many say that the two shells are more similar than different? More different than similar?" (Most students say the shells share more similarities). It is at this point that we reveal the different geographic origins of the shells, concluding, "Even though their origins are half a world apart, the shells are more alike than different."

2. Play the role of someone culturally different. At this point, excuse yourself from your classroom, pretending that you left something for your lesson at the copy machine or in the teachers' lounge. Don your robe or pajamas and reenter your room solemnly, reading aloud "What to Wear?" (see page 154). When you finish reading, say, "Imagine my embarrassment!"

3. Involve students in role plays. Tell students that you will need some volunteers as you introduce them to some other cultural differences. Use the following situations. They are also described in the book *I Felt Like I Was from Another Planet*:

- Invite two students to join you in eating some soup. Have each student take a bowl and spoon and begin to "eat" the soup. However, instead of using a spoon, you simply pick up your bowl and dig in. And, instead of eating quietly, slurp as loudly as you can. Then ask your students: "What's so funny? What did I do wrong?" Explain that in some cultures it is polite to make noises as you eat. If you have Dresser's book, read "Slurping" to your students at this point.

- Pick up one instrument. Tell students that you're very nervous because this is your first solo concert. Begin to play; your first "plant" should hoot and howl joyously. As this occurs, put your instrument down. After the noisy student has quieted down, pick up the next instrument. Repeat the process, with you playing and your "plant" hollering enthusiastic praise. Then, on the third instrument, have your second "plant" intervene, telling the howler to leave the concert immediately. Then ask your stu-

dents: "What's happening here? Who's right? Who's wrong?" Explain that in some cultures concertgoers are expected to sing, shout, and move along with the music. If you have Dresser's book, read "El Grito," the story of a girl whose newly arrived Mexican father doesn't know he is not supposed to make joyous noises (*gritos*) during his daughter's concert, since this behavior is appropriate in Mexico.

Optional: You may want to role-play or share other stories from *I Felt Like I Was from Another Planet*: embarrassment at not knowing the rules of baseball at recess; discomfort at being touched on the shoulder by an adult; gratefulness toward a classmate who offers sympathy to a child who wears white, the color of mourning a lost parent in China.

4. Discuss feelings about cultural differences. Ask your students how they think the characters you and the "plants" were portraying felt after the embarrassing moments. Then ask: "Who has experienced something similar? What happened? How did you feel?" If you wish, share with students the examples of cultural differences described in "Different Cultures, Different Ways" (see page 153). Finally, ask students the point of this lesson. No doubt, they'll have begun to see the influence of culture on behaviors. An added bonus: Students will recognize that they have survived embarrassing moments and lived to tell about them!

5. Challenge students to learn more. End the lesson with a return to your natural objects, reminding students again of their different origins. Then invite students to find someone in the class, school, family, or neighborhood who may have experienced some "culture shock" upon coming to a new setting. Ask students to choose a way to share their discoveries with the class. This may be a poster, brochure, skit, puppet play, or some other medium.

For Surefire Success

- If possible, try to find a copy of *I Felt Like I Was from Another Planet*. It is one of the best books available to help students appreciate cultural idiosyncrasies – their own and those of other people. In the book, more than 20 young immigrants to the U.S. discuss how their own cultures' mores and traditions caused them some social troubles upon arrival in the U.S. You can conduct this activity without the book, but having it will enhance the lesson.

- Locate additional resources (books, videos, speakers) that emphasize the unique contributions of different cultures. You will find some great examples of cultural do's and don'ts in the business section of any bookstore, where there are a variety of books that give hints to Western business travelers on how to interact in other cultures.

Classroom Extension

For those students who follow up your challenge to learn more, invite them to plan and participate in a panel discussion to be held in your classroom. Ask the panel to talk about what they have learned from others about the common bonds that unite us all and the uncommon behaviors that make each culture unique.

School Extensions

- Put on a "Cultural Road Show" where students reenact for other classes some of the stories in Dresser's book, in other sources, or from their own experience. Include in the event discussions in each classroom about how students can help newly arrived children from feeling embarrassed or out of place.

- Sponsor a "Cultural Fair" open to your community, in which people representing different cultures and traditions share food, traditional dress, music, art, lifestyles, and beliefs in an informative evening of fun. (One of our local schools did this, resulting in more than 2,500 community members attending the cultural exchange.)

Different Cultures, Different Ways

Many people from Latin American countries view a hug the way people from the U.S. view a handshake.

In the U.S., we feel comfortable with a good deal of "personal space" (at least two feet) between us and someone we're speaking with. People in China and the Middle East tend to stand at a distance of only a few inches.

Although a firm handshake is customary in the U.S., to many people from the Middle East and Europe, a too-firm handshake is considered aggressive and rude.

Americans give a "thumbs-up" when things are going well. This could be highly offensive to someone from Australia, where the gesture is considered obscene.

In China and Japan, visitors always exchange small gifts.

In many Latino and Native American cultures, children are expected *not* to look adults in the eye; doing so is a sign of disrespect.

Showing the soles of your shoes is considered an insult in Turkey and many Asian countries.

What to Wear?

I could hardly hear my little tummy crying of hunger. It was cold and we were in a small boat that was crowded with 100 men, women, and children. For four days, our boat seemed to be nowhere. All four of us, my three brothers and I, were squeezed next to our mother. We had shortage of food and water but none of us could eat or drink because whatever we took in, we threw up.

Children were crying and men were screaming, "Throw them off and feed them to the sharks!" It was a nightmare. We were escaping Communist Vietnam in hope of finding a safe place to live peacefully. We were lucky that we got to stay in the camps in Hong Kong for a year, and six months in the Philippine Islands. Finally, there was hope. The news came that our aunt was sponsoring us to come to America, the land of the free, the richest nation in the world.

The plane landed. My aunt and her husband drove two cars to pick up the nine of us and take us to their home. That is when I decided to call myself the American name Tiffany. The very next day my aunt took us shopping at K-mart for new clothes. My mom picked out what I thought to be the most beautiful outfit that I ever saw. The price was $9.99. The outfit was white, covered with pretty red, yellow, and pink flowers. The shirt had two front pockets where I could put my hands for warmth. I couldn't have been happier, and I was all smiles all through the day.

One month later, my aunt took my brothers and me to register for school. We were so excited that we all wore our new clothes because we had never attended school before. Although I was nine years old, I was placed in the first grade. I thought I was the best looking kid in school with two long pigtails that hung all the way to my small waist. I had on black cloth shoes, the kind that you might find in Chinatown, and I wore them without socks.

I entered the class and all eyes were shooting at my direction. All of a sudden, I felt like an alien from another planet. Even the teacher was staring at me with a funny look. I don't remember her, but the color of her hair was totally different from mine. To me it was like the color of the sun. I was so much smaller and shorter than all the other kids, but I felt even smaller right then. I wondered what made them so much bigger and taller than me.

The silence was broken by the teacher when she greeted me and guided me to an empty desk next to a dark-skinned girl with curly hair. She was very pretty with big eyes and long lashes. She smiled but I was speechless.

Moments later I saw someone of my culture talking to the teacher. Then that person, a female, approached me and asked in Chinese, "Why are you wearing your pajamas to school?" I didn't say anything and didn't understand why I wasn't supposed to wear what I was wearing to school. To me, pajamas are torn with patches and made of bad materials that make it uneasy for you to sleep in, not something that is so soft and comfortable that was 100% cotton.

I don't remember what happened after that very embarrassing day, but I never wore those so-called pajamas to school again. When I think back right now, the incident seems very amusing. How was I to know that it was wrong to wear what I wore to school that day? I guess it would be the same for anybody else from a totally different background.

From *I Felt Like I Was from Another Planet: Writing from Personal Experience* by Norine Dresser. Copyright © 1994 by Addison-Wesley Publishing Company. Reprinted by permission.

Index

About the Authors

Deb Delisle has been an educator for more than 25 years. Currently the Associate Superintendent of the Cleveland Heights-University Heights School District in Ohio, Deb has also been a primary teacher, gifted education teacher, public school administrator, and university instructor. Deb has been listed in *Who's Who Among American Teachers*, was a finalist for the Ohio Teacher of the Year, and was selected as one of America's Top Twenty Educators by *Learning Magazine* and the Oldsmobile Corporation.

Deb was a committee member of the National Board for Professional Teaching Standards, and she frequently conducts workshops for educators on curriculum development, global awareness, and alternative assessment.

Jim Delisle, Ph.D., has been a Professor of Education at Kent State University in Ohio for 25 years and currently directs the gifted-child education programs at both the undergraduate and graduate levels. He also teaches gifted middle school students part-time in Twinsburg, Ohio.

Jim is the author and coauthor of over 200 articles and books, including *More Than a Test Score* and *Smart Talk* (with Robert Schultz), *When Gifted Kids Don't Have All the Answers* and *The Gifted Kids' Survival Guide: A Teen Handbook* (with Judy Galbraith), *The Survival Guide for Teachers of Gifted Kids* (with Barbara Lewis), and *Once Upon a Mind: The Stories and Scholars of Gifted Child Education*. His work has been featured in the *New York Times*, *Washington Post*, and *People*, and on National Public Radio and O*prah*.

Deb and Jim split their time between their homes in Kent, Ohio, and North Myrtle Beach, South Carolina. They are proud parents of a grown-up gifted son, Matt, who resides and works in northern California. They wish he visited more often (hint, hint, Matt!).

Other Great Books from Free Spirit

The Complete Guide to Service Learning
Proven, Practical Ways to Engage Students in Civic Responsibility, Academic Curriculum, & Social Action
by Cathryn Berger Kaye, M.A.
Activities, quotes, reflections, resources, hundreds of annotated "Bookshelf" recommendations, and author interviews are presented within a curricular context and organized by theme to help teachers and youth workers engage young hearts and minds in reaching out and giving back. For teachers, grades K–12. *$29.95; 240 pp.; softcover; illust.; 8½" x 11"*

The Free Spirit Service Learning for Kids Series
by Cathryn Berger Kaye, M.A.
Put service learning into students' hands with these inspiring workbooks. Each focuses on a specific topic kids care about and overflows with ideas, facts, stories about real people helping others, resources, tips, and activities to motivate young people to take action in their own communities. The goal of each book is to help kids develop their skills, knowledge, and abilities while having a successful service-learning experience. Use with *The Complete Guide to Service Learning,* or use independently in a classroom or youth-serving organization. For grades 6 and up.
A Kids' Guide to Hunger & Homelessness
A Kids' Guide to Helping Others Read & Succeed
Each Book: $6.95; 48 pp.; softcover; illust.; 8½" x 11"

The Bully Free Classroom™
Over 100 Tips and Strategies for Teachers K–8
by Allan L. Beane, Ph.D.
Positive and practical, this solution-filled book can make any classroom a place where all students are free to learn without fear. It spells out 100 proven strategies teachers can start using immediately. Includes true stories, checklists, resources, and reproducible handout masters. For teachers, grades K–8. *$24.95; 176 pp.; softcover; 8½" x 11"*
The Bully Free Classroom™ CD-ROM
All of the forms, surveys, handouts, and letters from the book, ready to customize and print out.
$17.95, Macintosh and Windows compatible.

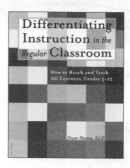

Differentiating Instruction in the Regular Classroom
How to Reach and Teach All Learners, Grades 3–12
by Diane Heacox, Ed.D.
Differentiation means changing the pace, level, or kind of instruction to fit the learner. This timely, practical guide is a menu of strategies, examples, templates, and tools teachers can use to differentiate instruction in any curriculum, even a standard or mandated curriculum, and ensure that every child has opportunities to learn and develop his or her talents. Includes dozens of reproducible handout masters. For teachers, grades 3–12. *$29.95; 176 pp.; softcover; 8½" x 11"*

Quick and Lively Classroom Activities
Meaningful Ways to Keep Kids Engaged During Transition Time, Downtime, or Anytime
by Linda Nason McElherne, M.A.
260 brief, enjoyable activities perfect for advisory, homeroom, or "between" times too short for something big and too long to waste. Grouped into 52 themes (one for each week of the year), each takes 15–20 minutes. The CD-ROM features all of the reproducible forms from the book, ready to print for classroom use. For teachers, grades 3–6. *$29.95; 184 pp.; softcover; illust.; 8½" x 11"*

Laughing Lessons
149⅔ Ways to Make Teaching and Learning Fun
by Ron Burgess
What's one of the best ways to get through to kids in your classroom? Lighten up! Even if you think you might be "humor impaired," this book can help you make your classroom a fun and lively place. If you take your job very seriously, this book is for you. For grades K–5.
$21.95; 208 pp.; softcover; illust.; 8" x 10"

Differentiating Content for Gifted Learners in Grades 6–12
A CD-ROM of Customizable Extensions Menus and Study Guides
by Susan Winebrenner
More than 140 reproducible forms and templates, plus detailed explanations on how to differentiate instruction for gifted and high-ability learners across a broad range of academic topics: literature, writing, history, social studies, math, science, health, foreign languages, and technology. Unique, timely, and ready to use, this stand-alone CD-ROM is a must-have tool for today's challenging classroom. For teachers, grades 6–12. *$21.95, Macintosh and Windows compatible*

To place an order or to request a free catalog of SELF-HELP FOR KIDS® and SELF-HELP FOR TEENS® materials, please write, call, email, or visit our Web site:

Free Spirit Publishing Inc.
217 Fifth Avenue North • Suite 200 • Minneapolis, MN 55401-1299
toll-free 800.735.7323 • local 612.338.2068 • fax 612.337.5050
help4kids@freespirit.com • www.freespirit.com